P O C K E T
S M I L E S

The Best in Wholesome Reading
CHOICE BOOKS Dept. 243
11923 Lee Highway
Fairfax, VA 22030
We Welcome Your Response

The Best in Wholesome Reading

CHOICE BOOKS Dept. 243

We Welcome Your Response

POCKET
SMILES
ROBERT C.
SAVAGE

Tyndale House
Publishers, Inc.
Wheaton, Illinois

Library of Congress Catalog Card Number 83-51243
ISBN 0-8423-4906-5, paper
Copyright © 1984 by Robert C. Savage
All rights reserved
Printed in the United States of America

12   93

Fifty years in the ministry of the gospel! During this half century I have been pastor or assistant pastor in many different churches (East Moline, and Harvey, Illinois; Pontiac, Romeo, Washington, Muskegon, and Haslett, Michigan; Washington, D.C.; Chinacota, Colombia; and Quito, Ecuador). But in my fiftieth year it was my special joy to minister to the wonderful people of the Sunny Isle Baptist Church in St. Croix (one of the U.S. Virgin Islands). They are great in many ways, and I appreciate the way they have responded to these "smiles".

Let's admit it, some of these 777 *Pocket Smiles* are "moldy oldies"; but whether old or new, they have made people laugh heartily when they heard them. In recognition of the church's warm-hearted encouragement and delightful fellowship in Christ, I dedicate this book of *Pocket Smiles*.

ROBERT C. SAVAGE

"A little nonsense now and then is relished by
  the best of men."

"Healthy people laugh and smile, making life
  much more worthwhile."

To make a smile come, so they say,
  brings fifteen muscles into play.
But if you want a frown to thrive
  you have to use some sixty-five!

When someone blushes with embarrassment,
When some heart carries away an ache,
When something sacred is made to appear
  common,
When somebody's weakness provides the
  laughter,
When profanity is required to make it funny,
When a little child is brought to tears, or
When everyone cannot join in the laughter—
  It's a poor joke.

The above were suggested for *Pocket Smiles* by
Howard Schoof, who has graciously cooperated

as consulting editor in producing the three books, *Pocket Quips, Pocket Wisdom,* and *Pocket Smiles.* Howard and I have exchanged "smiles" since 1938 when we were fellow students at Moody Bible Institute. What a delightful sense of humor he has, combined with a philosophy of life that is profoundly stimulating—intellectually and spiritually.

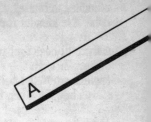

ABSENT-MINDED

One of the world's greatest scientists was also recognized as the original absent-minded professor. One day, on board a train, he was unable to find his ticket. The conductor said, "Take it easy. You'll find it."

When the conductor returned, the professor still couldn't find the ticket. The conductor, recognizing the famous scientist, said, "I'm sure you bought a ticket. Forget about it."

"You're very kind," he said, "but I must find it, otherwise I won't know where to get off."

She: "I wonder if you remember me? Years ago you asked me to marry you."
Professor: "Ah yes . . . and did you?"

Professor (sitting beside his bed with a shoe in his hand): "Let's see, am I going to sleep or waking up?"

Professor Jones was visiting a ranch out in Texas. He looked at a rope in his hand and

mumbled to himself, "One of two things—
either I've found a rope or lost a horse."

Friend: "I hear your wife had twins. Were they
boys or girls?"
Professor: "Well, I believe one is a girl and one
is a boy, but it may be the other way around."

Maid (to professor who was sick): "Professor,
the doctor is here."
Professor: "Dear me! I'm in bed. I can't see
him. Er—tell him I'm ill."

The university professor and his wife were
leaving church.
Professor: "Ha, ha! Who's absent-minded now?
You forgot your umbrella and left it in
church, but I remembered mine and I picked
up yours, too."
Wife: "Fine—but the trouble is, neither you
nor I brought an umbrella to church today!"

An absent-minded professor met an old friend
as he was walking along the street. They
conversed for about fifteen minutes and were
ready to say farewell.

The professor asked, "Do you remember—
was I going toward the college or away from
the college when we met?"

"You were going toward the college."

"Oh, thanks. That means I've had my lunch."

One morning as he was leaving for the university
his wife told her absent-minded husband,

"Don't forget we are moving today. If you come to this house this afternoon it will be empty."

Predictably he didn't remember until he found the house vacated that afternoon. He mumbled to himself, "And where was it we were moving to?"

He went out in front of the house and asked a little girl, "Did you see a moving van here today?"

"Yes," she replied.

"Would you know which way it went?"

She looked up at him and said, "Yes, Daddy, I'll show you."

AGE

Husband: "Ann, do you remember Jim Williams? He was president of our senior class at high school."

Ann: "That was 35 years ago."

Husband: "You're right. Anyhow, he has gotten so bald and so fat that he didn't even recognize me."

A young man was asked to guess the age of the hostess at the party. With a tactful smile he said, "I have several ideas, but I'm trying to decide whether to make you 10 years younger on account of your looks or 10 years older on account of your intelligence."

(See also: Old Age, Birthdays)

AIRPLANES

The lady passenger became hysterical when she saw the flames licking engines 1 and 2: "We're on fire!" she shouted up and down the aisle. We're on fire! We're going to crash!"

The entire planeload of passengers was in panic. Suddenly the pilot appeared wearing a parachute. "Please be calm, everyone; don't worry about a thing," he assured them. "I'm going for help."

Little Johnny was having a terrific time on his first plane trip. He pushed every button in sight, ran through the aisles at top speed and finally crashed into the stewardess as she was serving a tray of coffee.

The stewardess picked herself up and grabbed young Johnny by the arm. "Little boy," she cooed sweetly, "why don't you go outside and play?"

This jet age is absolutely amazing. You can have breakfast in London . . . lunch in New York . . . dinner in Los Angeles, and your suitcases in Buenos Aires!

Did you hear about that new aviation poison? One drop and you're dead!

An elderly woman flying for the first time was happy to see the pilot as he walked down the aisle greeting passengers and inspecting the aircraft.

"Sir," said the little old lady, "you'll bring me down safely, won't you?"

"Of course," the captain answered. "I've never left anyone up here yet."

One morning a man called a taxi company and complained that a cab he ordered to take him to the airport had not arrived. The girl who took the call apologized, "I'm very sorry the cab isn't there yet, sir, but don't worry, the plane is always late."

"Well, it certainly will be this morning," the caller said sharply, "I happen to be the pilot!"

The loudspeaker of the big jet clicked on and the captain's voice announced: "Now, there's no cause for alarm, but we felt that you should know for the last 2 hours we've been flying without the benefit of radio, compass, radar or navigational beam. This means I am not quite sure in which direction we are heading. However, I'm sure you'll be interested to know that we are making excellent time."

AMERICA

What America needs more than anything else is fewer people telling what America needs more than anything else.

APOLOGY

Carl had to apologize for forgetting his aunt's birthday. So he wrote her a letter. "I'm so sorry

I forgot your birthday. I have no excuse and it would serve me right if you forgot mine, which is next Friday."

ARMY

A draftee was assigned to the parachute outfit and received instructions for his first jump. The captain told him to pull the cord with his left hand after jumping. But if it didn't open, then he was to pull the cord with his right hand.

"There will be a truck to pick you up and bring you back," the instructor said.

The fellow jumped and pulled the cord with his left hand, but it didn't open. He pulled the other cord with his right hand, but it still didn't open.

He was heard to say, as he passed another parachutist on his way down, "Nothing works in this army so far and I'll bet that truck won't be there to pick me up either."

It's always good to know who you are speaking to as illustrated from this incident during the Vietnam War. The phone call went like this:

First Voice: "Would you check on whether a jeep has just pulled up in front of the barracks?"

Second Voice: "I'm too busy right now for something unimportant like that."

First Voice: "Do you know who this is?"

Second Voice: "No."

First Voice: "Well, this is General Westmoreland."

Second Voice: "Do you know who this is?"
First Voice: "No."
Second Voice: "Well then, good-bye, you old
  fathead!"

The paratroopers were being instructed on the
use of their chutes.
Rookie: "What if it doesn't open?"
Instructor: "That, my friend, is known as
  jumping to a conclusion!"

The 19-year-old was being inducted into the
army. The captain told him, "We're putting you
in the cavalry. Come with me and I'll show you
your horse."

At the stables the recruit was shown the tall,
gray horse and he tried to explain his situation.
"But, Captain, I've never ridden a horse before."

"No problem," replied the captain, "because
this horse has never been ridden before."

ART

Any great painting
will leave my wife fainting.
Its beauty so powerfully enthralls.
But never before
did she slump to the floor
as at Junior's new work on our walls!

It happened at an art exhibit. A couple of boys
came to a wild abstract painting. After looking it
over for a couple of minutes one of the kids

muttered to the other, "We'd better get out of here before they blame us for having done it."

Abstract Art: A product of the untalented, sold by the unprincipled, to the utterly bewildered. (Al Capp)

A painting in a musem hears more ridiculous opinions than anything else in the world.

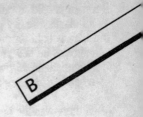

BABIES
People who say they sleep like a baby undoubtedly don't have one.

What is meant by "spitting image"? A Dad finds out the meaning when he tries to feed pabulum to his baby boy of 8 months.

BACHELOR
A bachelor is a man who never made the same mistake once.

A bachelor is one who is "foot-loose and fiancée-free."

BALDNESS
At a certain time of life a man's hair begins to grow inward. If it strikes gray matter it turns gray. If it doesn't strike anything it disappears.

"Now his head resembles heaven, for there is 'no parting there.' "

If a man is bald toward the front of his head
it indicates he is a great thinker.

If a man is bald toward the back of his head it
indicates he is a great lover.

If a man is bald all over his head it indicates
he just *thinks* he's a great lover.

Then there was the one about the bald-headed
fellow who took up the hobby of reading
mystery stories because they were hair raising!

BAPTISTS

There were two churches in the community, a
Methodist church and a Baptist church.

The Baptists were temporarily without a
pastor when a deacon of the church died. The
family asked the Methodist pastor if he would
conduct the funeral service.

This was his first year in the ministry and
the Methodist pastor felt he needed approval
from the bishop of the area. So he sent a
telegram asking: "May I have approval to bury
a Baptist deacon?"

The bishop quickly replied with a telegram
reading: "Bury all the Baptists you can!"

A woman went into a small town post office
recently and asked for five dollars' worth of
stamps.

"What denomination?" asked the clerk.

"Well," came the angry reply, "I didn't know
it would ever come to this, but if you nosey

18

government people have to know, I'm a Baptist!"

Two fellows were discussing the question how the Baptists originated.

First fellow: "That's easy! Anybody knows we Baptists got started with John the Baptist."

Second fellow: "You're wrong; the origin went back a lot further than that. Don't you remember when Abraham and Lot were surveying the land of Canaan? They walked together for a long time, over the hills, across the streams, through the valleys. Then Abraham said to Lot, 'All right, you go your way and I'll go mine.' That's when the Baptist denomination got started!"

There are 3 kinds of Baptists: The Baptists South of God; the Baptists North of God; and the Baptists Independent of God.

Charles Spurgeon's mother said, "Son, I prayed to the Lord that he would make you a Christian. But I didn't ask him to make you a Baptist."

Spurgeon: "Mother, that is only typical of the Lord's generosity. He always gives over and above all that we ask or think."

Note: The compiler of this book is a Baptist and believes one of the most healthy aspects of humor is to be able to laugh at yourself.

(See also: Deacons, Denominations)

BARBERS

Small wonder my barber has that rather happy smirk on his face. Each year his haircut price goes up and each year there's less to work on.

BEAUTY

She's still just as pretty, but it now takes her a half hour longer.

BIBLE

Sister Jones got out her Bible and decided she would let the Lord lead to the specific verse she needed for the day. So with eyes closed she opened her Bible and put her finger on a verse. Opening her eyes she read, "And Judas went out and hanged himself."

She quickly sought a different verse, once again closing her eyes and placing her finger on the specific spot. This time she was disappointed to read, "Go thou and do likewise!"

Undaunted she followed the same plan a third time, and the verse was, "What thou doest, do quickly!"

Who is the smallest man in the Bible? It was Peter. He slept on his watch.

Who was the most popular actor in the Bible? Samson. He brought down the house.

A woman was mailing the old family Bible to her brother in a distant city. The postal clerk

examined the heavy package carefully and
inquired if it contained anything breakable.
"Nothing except maybe the Ten Commandments," was the quick reply.

A pastor was making a visit. The mother wanting
to impress the pastor said to the daughter,
"Honey, bring me the book we read so much."
    The mother thought she would return with
the Bible, but to her dismay, the girl brought
the Sears, Roebuck catalogue.

King David and King Solomon lived merry,
    merry lives,
with many, many lady friends and many,
    many wives.
But when old age crept over them, with
    many, many qualms
King Solomon wrote the Proverbs, and
King David wrote the Psalms.

The youth director of Central Church discovered
that most of the teen-agers thought that an
"epistle" was the wife of an "apostle."

BIG SHOTS

Secretary concerning her boss: "You can't help
admiring him . . . if you don't, you're fired."

He's easily entertained. All we have to do is just
listen to him . . . hour after hour after hour.

He's a self-made man who adores his maker.

21

He's a self-made man who apparently knocked off work too soon.

He's a real big gun—small caliber and an immense bore.

Be careful when you talk about him, you're speaking of the man he loves.

He's all wrapped up in himself, and it makes a very small package.

Success turned his head . . . too bad it didn't wring his neck.

He's so proud, when he hears thunder, he takes a bow.

He claims to be the architect of his own success. Lucky the building inspectors didn't come around during the construction.

You could make a fortune if you could buy him for what *you* think of him, and sell him for what *he* thinks he's worth.

He who goes in circles shall be called a big wheel.

(See also: Conceit, Egotist)

BIRTHDAYS
She looks like a million—*every year of it!*

Forty has been the most difficult age for her to pass—in fact it has taken her 8 years!

If she put the right number of candles on her birthday cake, it would be a fire hazard.

She's celebrating the 10th anniversary of her 29th birthday.

When it comes to telling her age she is shy—about ten years shy.

Dinner's defrosting,
    Mother's not.
Today's her birthday,
    and Dad forgot!

Two husbands were talking things over. Warren (to Ken): "It's terrible to grow old alone . . . my wife hasn't had a birthday in 10 years!"

Distraught mother to group of wild children at birthday party: "Hey kids, there will be a special prize for the one who goes home first."

BOASTING

Harry was a sophomore in college. When he came home for vacation he was boasting to his neighbor about the great strength he had gained by doing a lot of weight lifting.

After listening to his bragging for a half hour Vic was fed up with it. He said, "Listen, young fellow, I'll bet you $25 I can wheel a load in this wheelbarrow to the other side of the street and you can't wheel it back."

"I'll sure take you on. What's your load going to be?"

"*You!* Get in."

BODY

It looks as though I was built wrong. My nose runs and my feet smell!

BOREDOM

He's very cultured. He can bore you on any subject.

BORROWING

The neighborhood borrower approached Mr. Smith Saturday morning and inquired: "Say, Smith, are you using your lawnmower this afternoon?"

"Yes, I am," Smith replied wearily.

"Fine, then you won't be needing your golf clubs. I'll just borrow them."

BOYS

At a football game Mervin was told, "Sit down in front!"

"I can't," he replied, "I'm not made that way."

Joey came home after his first day in school.

Mother: "How did you get along?"

Joey: "The teacher asked me a lot of questions."

Mother: "What for instance?"

Joey: "She wanted to know where I was born."

Mother: "What did you tell her?"

Joey: "It sounded too 'sissy' to say Women's Hospital, so I said Tiger Stadium."

BOWLING

I could have been a champion bowler, but it wasn't up my alley.

Did you hear about the preachers who organized a bowling team? They call themselves the *holy rollers.*

BUGS

Mama flea looked worried. When papa flea asked what was the matter, she replied, "Daddy, none of our children are going to the dogs."

BUREAUCRACY

A bureaucrat's idea of cleaning up his files is to make a copy of every paper before he destroys it.

Guidelines for bureaucrats: (1) When in charge ponder. (2) When in trouble delegate. (3) When in doubt mumble.

CAPITAL PUNISHMENT

Asked if he had any last words before going to the electric chair, the criminal replied, "This is sure going to be an everlasting lesson for me."

CATHOLICS

Have you heard of the new drive-in confessional plan? It is called, "Toot and tell!"

CEMETERIES

Epitaph on a tombstone:
Here lies my wife Samantha Proctor.
She had the flu and wouldn't doctor.
She couldn't stay; she had to go.
"Praise God from whom all blessings flow!"

CHAIN LETTERS

This chain letter is meant to bring happiness to you. Unlike other chain letters it does not cost money. Just send a copy of this letter to 6 other churches who are tired of their ministers. Then bundle up your pastor and send him to the church at the bottom of the list. In one week you will receive 16,346 ministers, and one of them should be a dandy. Have faith in this letter.

P.S. One church broke this chain . . . and they got their old minister back.

CHEERFULNESS

A good concoction to improve cheerfulness is a mixture of yeast and shoe polish. It enables us "to rise and shine."

CHICKENS

Some boys were playing football near a chicken yard. Accidently their white football got kicked into the yard where Mr. Rooster and about 20 hens were congregated.

Mr. Rooster went over to examine the big white egg. He called all the hens over to join in the examination. Then he spoke to them. "Now girls, I don't want to complain or find fault with you, but I want you to see what the competition is producing!"

The Reverend Henry Ward Beecher
    called a hen a most elegant creature.
The hen, pleased with that,
    laid an egg in his hat.
And thus did the hen reward Beecher!
(Oliver Wendell Homes)

CHILDREN

Policeman: "Little boy, why do you keep
running around the block?"

Little Boy: "I'm running away from home. But I
must stay on this side of the street because
Daddy says I shouldn't cross the street by
myself."

My mother loved children—she would have
given anything if I had been one.
(Groucho Marx)

Children are unpredictable. You never know
what inconsistency they're going to catch you
in next.

The persons hardest to convince they're at the
retirement age are children at bedtime.

Susie, age 4, had been put to bed upstairs.
Her daddy was in the living room, reading the
paper.

Susie called out from her bed: "Daddy, will
you bring me a drink of water?"

Dad: "No, Susie, you've already had your
drink of water."

Five minutes later she again called out:
"Daddy, will you bring me a drink of water?"

Dad: "No, Susie, you've had all you need.
Now go to sleep and don't call again."

Five minutes later there was a third call:
"Daddy, please bring me a drink of water."

Dad: "Now listen, Susie, if you don't quit

calling I'm going to come up and spank you."

Susie: "Daddy, when you come up to spank me will you bring me a drink of water?"

Our neighbors back in Pontiac had twins. They named one "Sears" and the other "Roebuck"—because they were of the "mail order."

A little girl was always falling out of bed. When a friend asked her why it was, she answered, "I guess it's because I sleep too close to where I get in."

Eight-year-old Tommy was invited to a neighbor's home for supper.

Neighbor lady: "Are you sure you can cut your meat, Tommy?"

Tommy: "Oh yes, thanks, We often have it just as tough as this at home."

"Eenie, meenie, minie, moe" is a phrase that inspired a husband and wife in naming their children.

The first-born they named "Eenie."

The second one they called "Meenie."

The name of the third was "Minie."

But when the fourth was born they called him "Elmer."

When a friend asked them for an explanation why they departed from the pattern of "Eenie, meenie, minie, moe," they explained, "We don't want any 'moe.'"

CHRISTIAN SCIENTISTS

One such was a teacher named Deal,
who said, "Although pain isn't real,
if I sit on a pin and it punctures my skin,
I dislike that I fancy I feel."

CHURCH

Several women were talking together. One
said, "Our congregation is sometimes down
to 30 or 40 on Sunday night."

Another said, "That's nothing, sometimes
our group is down to 6 or 7."

A young widow added her bit, "It's so bad
in our church on Sunday night that when the
minister says, 'Dearly beloved,' it makes me
think he's proposing."

A woman who "enjoyed her religion" visited a
very staid and formal church. "Amen" she said,
as the preacher brought out a point with which
she agreed.

"Madam," said the usher standing nearby,
"Please try and restrain yourself. We don't allow
that in this church."

In a few moments she was so carried away
by the sermon that she shouted, "Amen, praise
the Lord, hallelujah!"

The usher rushed to her side: "Madam! You
must quiet down immediately or leave!"

"I didn't mean to disturb . . . but I am just so
happy since I found the Lord," she explained.

"You may have found the Lord," retorted the

usher severely, "but I am quite sure you didn't find him here!"

I'm a First United Presbytalian Metho-Bapto-Gationalist.

"I am building a church," said a small boy playing with a set of blocks, "and we must be very quiet."
His father eager to encourage this unexpected reverence, asked: "Why are we to be quiet in church?"
"Because the people are asleep," was the boy's response.

A boy stopped before a large bronze plaque in the foyer of the big church. "What are all those names up there?" he asked the minister.
"Those, sonny," the minister answered, "are the names of people who died in the service."
"Which one?" asked the little boy. "The morning or the evening service?"

The following have been gathered from various church bulletins:

"Ladies, don't forget the rummage sale. It's a good chance to get rid of those things not worth keeping around the house. Bring your husbands."

Sermon—"Gossip."
Invitation hymn—"I Love to Tell the Story."

There will be no healing service this Sunday due to the pastor's illness.

The Clinic for Soul-Sinning will be held Friday at 7:30 P.M.

This afternoon there will be a meeting in the north and south ends of the church. Children will be baptized at both ends.

(See also: Preachers, Sermons)

COLLEGE

His brother has a Ph.D.
His wife has an M.A.
His daughter has a B.A.
He is the only one with a J.O.B.

College dean (to his wife): "I'm going to stop this necking on the campus."
Wife: "A man of your age ought to."

Bill: "But officer, have pity, I'm a college student."
Policeman: "Sorry, but I've got to give a ticket. *Ignorance* is no excuse."

At its 20th reunion a Princeton class discovered that it had gained two and a half tons of weight!

Professor to class: "If you get this in your head, you'll have it in a nutshell."

As they gathered for chapel service the college dean took a few minutes to give the student body a much needed scolding. "The kissing and petting that is taking place on this campus is

32

absolutely disgraceful. It is shocking. Why some of it is going on right under my nose!"

Sophomore: "Prof, I'm so sorry I'm late. I'll be bright and early tomorrow."

Professor: "Don't promise too much. Just be here early."

It was the night before final exams and everyone was cramming in preparation. One fellow was almost a nervous wreck as he paced the floor. He would snap his fingers and call out, "B-a-i-k, b-a-i-k."

A fellow student interrupted him, "What does b-a-i-k mean?"

"It means *boy am I konfused.*"

"But *confused* should be spelled with a 'c' not a 'k,' " suggested his friend.

The distraught student snapped his fingers again saying, "Boy, I'm more confused than I thought I was!"

When asked for the most beautiful words in the English language, this sophomore answered: "Check enclosed."

(See also: Professors, Schools, Teachers)

COMMITTEES

A pastor met with his board of trustees and requested they approve the purchase of a chandelier for the church sanctuary. The next month when the minutes were read there was

33

no mention of the pastor's suggestion, so he requested it a second time.

The third month the pastor waited expectantly for a report of action taken, but there was absolutely no word in the minutes of his request. So after the meeting he went to the chairman of the board and asked for an explanation.

"Well, pastor, it was this way," explained the chairman. "First of all, the secretary of the trustees didn't know how to spell the word, and it would have embarrassed him if we had insisted on it being included in the minutes. Second, if we got one of those things, we don't believe there is anyone in the church who knows how to play it. And third, we feel that as concerns the church sanctuary, the thing we really need is better lighting."

Committee—a group of men who individually can do nothing but as a group decide that nothing can be done.

COMPUTERS

A man in Wichita, Kansas, received a computerized bill. The balance due column read $00.00. He threw it away.

A month later the same store sent another bill with the following notation: "This balance is now past due." He circled the zeros and sent the bill back to the store.

A few days later he received another

scorching computerized letter. It admonished him to pay his debt of $00.00. Realizing that nothing can be quite as stubborn as a computer, he finally sat down and wrote out a check for $00.00. He received no further bills from the store.

CONCEIT

Egotist: "I don't think I'm great, but what is my opinion against the whole world?"

He could hardly wait to hear what he was going to say.

Egotist: "I'm so glad I'm not conceited like other great men."

(See also: Big Shots, Egotist)

CORRECTION

The town newspaper included an article that stated, "Half of the city council are crooks."

A storm of protest resulted, so the editor issued the following correction: "Half of the city council are not crooks."

COWBOYS

Cowboy: "How much are your spurs?"
Clerk: "Ten dollars a pair."
Cowboy: "Here's $5. Give me one."
Clerk: "What can you do with one spur?"

Cowboy: "Well, I figure if I get one side of the horse going, the other side will keep up."

CRITICISM

If you must throw cold water on everything, then get a job as a fireman.

CRAZY QUIZ

1. Where was Paul going on the road to Damascus?
2. From what animal do we get whale bones?
3. In what year was the battle of 1812 fought?
4. Do they have a 4th of July in England?
5. Why did Moses take two caterpillars with him into the Ark?
6. Of what state is Springfield, Illinois, the capital?
7. If you go to bed at 8 P.M. and set the alarm to get up at 9 A.M., how many hours can you sleep before the alarm wakes you up?
8. Some months have 30 days, some have 31 days. How many months have 28 days?
9. Who wrote the Gospel according to Mark?
10. Why can't a man living in Winston-Salem, North Carolina, be buried west of the Mississippi River?
11. A farmer had 17 sheep. All but 9 died. How many does he have left?
12. Take 2 apples from 3 apples and what do you have?
13. If f-o-l-k spells folk, how do you spell the white of an egg?

14. If a rooster laid an egg on the top of a hill, which side would the egg roll down?

15. How many birthdays does an average man have?

16. An archaeologist claimed he found some gold coins in Italy dated 46 B.C. Is he reliable?

17. What word in this test is mispelled?

Answers

1. Damascus   2. Whales   3. 1812   4. Yes
5. It wasn't Moses, it ws Noah.   6. Illinois   7. One hour
8. All 12   9. Mark   10. He must die first.   11. Nine
12. Two apples   13. W-h-i-t-e   14. Roosters don't lay eggs.   15. One   16. No—B.C. wasn't used until after Christ.   17. Misspelled

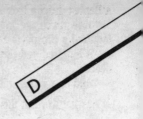

DADS

Larry: "Dad, did God make you?"
Dad: "Yes."
Larry: "And did he make me?"
Dad: "Yes."
Larry: "He's doing better work lately, eh?"

DAYLIGHT-SAVING TIME

The idea for daylight-saving time came from an Indian chief who cut off one end of his blanket and sewed it on the other end so he could make the blanket longer.

DEACONS

Whenever there was a testimony meeting Deacon Davis would participate. Each time he would conclude his testimony with, "Friends, I'm aiming to do better."

After about 15 such testimonies the pastor observed, "Deacon Davis, I think it's about time you were pulling the trigger!"

A Baptist deacon had advertised a cow for sale.

"How much are you asking for her?" inquired a prospective purchaser.

"A hundred and fifty dollars," said the deacon.

"And how much milk does she give?"

"Four gallons a day," he replied.

"But how do I know that she will actually give that amount?" asked the prospective purchaser.

"Oh, you can trust me," reassured the advertiser, "I'm a Baptist deacon."

"I'll buy her then," replied the other. "I'll take her home and bring you back the money later. You can trust me, I'm a Presbyterian elder."

When the deacon arrived home he asked his wife, "What is a Presbyterian elder?"

"Oh," she replied, "a Presbyterian elder is about the same as a Baptist deacon."

"Oh, dear," groaned the deacon, "I'll never get my money!"

DEATH

Dying is the last thing I ever intend to do.

It was a small town on Sunday morning. When the minister arrived at the church he saw a dead mule in the driveway, a victim of a Saturday night accident. The preacher went to the phone and called the mayor.

"Why tell me?" asked the mayor. "I thought you preachers buried the dead."

"We do," answered the preacher, "but first we always like to notify the next of kin." (Luella Dahlstrom)

A fellow had this inscribed upon his tombstone, "I expected this, but not just yet."

A Dad promised to buy his boy a puppy. So they went to the dog kennel to look over the ones that were for sale. When the Dad asked the boy which puppy he wanted, he pointed to a pup that constantly wagged his tail, and said, "I want that one with the happy ending."

I'm not afraid to die. I just don't want to be there when it happens. (Woody Allen)

DECEIT
"I know you aren't two-faced," said Merv to Harold, "because if you were, you'd wear the other one!"

DEER HUNTING
Once 2 hunters got lost in the forest. The first hunter said, "Now we must be calm."

The second hunter agreed, "You're right. I once read that if you get lost you should shoot 3 times into the air and someone will come and rescue you."

So they did this, but nothing happened. They did it again, but still no help came. They repeated this several times without results.

Finally the first hunter said, "What are we going to do now?"

And the second hunter replied, "I don't know. We're almost out of arrows."

DEMONSTRATORS

Demonstrator No. 1: "There's one thing about this 'down with the government' demonstration that worries me."

Demonstrator No. 2: "And what's that?"

Demonstrator No. 1: "How are we going to get our unemployment checks and food stamps after we overthrow this lousy government?"

DENOMINATIONS

Two churches in a small town were contemplating a merger. One was a Baptist church and the other a Christian church. Approval of the plan was almost unanimous. But one old-timer objected.

"No," he said, as he shook his head.

"Why, sir?" he was asked.

"Well, my mother and father were Baptists, my grandparents were Baptists, all of my people were Baptists . . . and nobody is going to make a Christian out of me now!"

Bryce: "What are you?"

Ed: "I'm a Methodist."

Bryce: "Why?"

Ed: "Because my mother and dad were Methodists."

Bryce: "That's not a very good reason. Let's say your mother and dad had been Baptists, what would you be?"
Ed: "A moron!"

(See also: Baptists)

DENTISTS

Jones had a toothache, so he decided to go to the dentist.
Jones: "How much do you charge for pulling a tooth?"
Dentist: "$20."
Jones: "$20 for only 5 minutes work?"
Dentist: "Well, if you wish, I can extract it very slowly."

It is easy enough to be happy
when life is a bright, rosy wreath.
But the man worthwhile
is the man who can smile
when the dentist is filling his teeth.

DICTATORS

The dictator of a small country was bitterly disappointed that nobody would use the newly-issued postage stamps bearing his portrait. He questioned a postmaster, who explained that the stamps weren't sticking.

Seizing one, the dictator licked it and stuck it to an envelope. "Look!" he shouted. "It sticks perfectly!"

The postmaster faltered for a moment, then explained, "Well, sir, the truth is that the people have been spitting on the wrong side."

DID YOU HEAR?

"Did you hear about the rope joke?"
"No."
"Skip it!"

"Did you hear about the coed who when she went to college found out that she wasn't the only pebble on the beach?"
"No, what happened?"
"She became a little bolder."

Did you hear that they're building a $20 million hotel right in the heart of Moscow? They're going to call it the "Comrade Hilton."

"Did you hear the story about the dirty window?"
"No, I didn't."
"Well, that's OK. You couldn't see through it anyhow!"

Did you hear about the fellow who had an awful nightmare? He dreamed he was forced by cruel men to eat and swallow a 6-pound marsh-mallow. When he awoke the next morning he noticed his pillow was missing.

Did you hear about the elevator operator who got fired? He couldn't remember the route!

Did you hear about the guy who was so dumb it wasn't until he had used Right Guard for 2 months he learned he could also use it under his left arm?

Did you hear about the man who first met his wife at a travel bureau? She was looking for a vacation and he was the last resort!

DID YOU KNOW?

Did you know why women's minds are cleaner than men's? It's because they change them so often!

Did you know what the skunk said when the wind turned? "It all comes back to me now!"

Did you know that 50 percent of the passengers who fly from London to Paris go by air?

DIETING

My wife is on a diet—coconuts and bananas. She hasn't lost any weight, but boy, can she ever climb trees!

Diets are for people who are "thick and tired" of it.

DIPLOMACY

Her husband is a real diplomat. He always remembers her birthday, but forgets what her age is.

DOCTORS

Isn't it interesting the way we talk about
pastors—ministering;
professors—teaching; and
doctors—practicing?

Mrs. Brunner to doctor: "It's so good of you,
doctor, to have come this far to see my
husband."

Dr. Cramer: "Not at all, Mrs. Brunner. I have
another patient next door, and I thought I
might as well kill two birds with one stone."

Patient: "Doctor, my right foot is killing me."
Doctor: "Oh, I imagine it's just old age."
Patient: "Old age? But doctor, my left foot is
just as old. How come it doesn't hurt?"

Margaret: "I had an operation and the doctor
left a sponge in me."
Wanda: "That's awful. Do you have a lot of
pain?"
Margaret: "No, but it's terrible how thirsty I
am all the time."

Doctor: "Say, the check you gave me for my
doctor bill came back."
Patient: "Yeah, and so did my arthritis!"

Report on Grandma Mitchell: "She's near
death's door and the doctor hopes he can pull
her through."

After addressing the gathering the speaker, who
was a well-known physician, asked the reporters

to not publish any of his speech because he planned to give the same lecture in a neighboring town in a few days.

The next day the doctor was horrified to read in the local paper: "Dr. Smith delivered an excellent lecture. He told some wonderful stories. Unfortunately they cannot be published."

A pretty teen-age girl to doctor listening to her heart: "Doctor, does it sound broken?"

DRIVING

Police officer: "Hey, lady, pull over. Do you know you were doing 70?"

Pretty woman: "Isn't that marvelous? And I just learned to drive yesterday!"

Safety slogan: Look out for school children—especially if they are driving cars.

A couple of motorists met on a bridge not wide enough for two cars to pass.

"I never back up for an idiot!" yelled one driver.

"That's all right," said the other as he shifted into reverse, "I always do."

Every year it takes less time to fly across the ocean and more time to drive to the office. (Raymond Duncan)

Abraham Lincoln declared you can't fool all the people all the time, but these highway interchange signs come pretty close.

A dashing young fellow named Tim drove his
car with a great deal of vim.
Said he, "I'm renowned
for covering ground."
But alas, now the ground covers him.

DRUNKS

He was heading home, but needed some excuse
to tell his wife why he was intoxicated again.
Pausing in front of a music store he noticed
the word *syncopation*.

"That's a good idea," he mumbled to
himself, "I'll tell her I've been afflicted with
syncopation."

When he encountered his wife at the door of
their home he gave that excuse. She didn't know
what *syncopation* was, so she got out the
dictionary. The definition she found was:
"erratic hopping from bar to bar."

As he boarded the plane for a flight to Phoenix,
the priest resolved that he would give a witness
of his faith to whomever would be sitting beside
him. However, the one who sat down next to
him was drunk, and the priest dispaired of
being able to give a very effective witness.

The drunk unfolded a newspaper and
started reading. After a few minutes he turned
to the priest saying, "Hey, mister, can you tell
me why a person gets arthritis?"

Here's my opportunity, thought the priest
to himself. "Arthritis is the result of drinking,
carousing and bad companions," he carefully

explained to his intoxicated companion. "But why did you ask?"

"Oh, I was just reading here that the Archbishop of Chicago is suffering from arthritis."

'Twas late in November
(the date I can't remember),
I was leading home a manly jag with pride,
When my feet began to stutter
and I fell down in the gutter
and a pig came up and laid down by my side.
It always is fair weather
when good friends get together,
and a lady passing by was heard to say,
"You can tell the one who boozes, by the
company he chooses."
And the pig got up, and quickly walked away.

Bleary-eyed he approached a pedestrian and asked, "Shay, mister, could you tell me where the other shide of the street is?"
Pedestrian: "Yes, it's right over there."
Drunk: "No, it isn't. I was just over there and a guy told me it was over here someplace."

Two drunks were walking along a railroad track. One said, "These are the widest steps I ever walked up in my life."

The other drunk said, "It's not the wide steps that are killing me. It's this low handrail."

Did you hear about the Swede who went into a bar and asked if they had any Green Frog whiskey?

Bartender: "We don't have any Green Frog whiskey, but how about some Old Crow whiskey?"

Swede: "Oh no, no—I don't vant to fly, I yust vant to yump around a little bit!"

A local minister coming home late from a sick call saw one of his parishioners staggering out of the bar. He offered to take the inebriated friend home. When they got to the fellow's door, the preacher bid him good-night, but the intoxicated member grabbed him by the arm.

"Pleash, reverend, come inside for jusht a minute. I want my wife to shee who I've been out with tonight."

EARLY

A mother tried to awaken her 6-year-old son so he could get on his way to school. Finally he half-opened his eyes, looked at her with disgust and remarked, "Whoever invented morning sure made it too early."
(Jacqueline Ahlstrand)

We may not understand much about the speed of light, but we have discovered one thing about it, it gets here *too* early in the morning.

ECONOMY

Just about the time you think you can make ends meet, someone moves the ends!

EDUCATION

A divinity student named Fiddle,
refused to accept his degree.
'Tis enough, said he, to be Fiddle,
without being Fiddle D.D.

EGOTIST

Every year he takes a "boast-to-boast" tour.

If he had his life to live over again, he would still fall in love with himself.

(See also: Big Shots, Conceit)

EMBARRASSING MOMENTS

Sam Richardson picked up the wrong umbrella as he was leaving the restaurant and the right owner called his attention to it. Sam was dreadfully embarrassed and offered red-faced apologies.

But the incident reminded him that he had promised to buy umbrellas for both his wife and his daughter. So he purchased one for each of them, along with one for himself.

As he walked out of the store heading for his car, he saw the fellow whose umbrella he had accidently picked up at the restaurant. The man eyed him suspiciously and said, "I see you had a good day after all."

When Pastor Brown saw Sister Webster coming toward the door of the parsonage he said to his wife, "You take care of her. I can't be bothered with her tireless talk. I'll go upstairs and study."

Two hours later he yelled from upstairs, "Hey, honey, has that old bore left yet?"

Sister Webster was still there, but the pastor's wife cleverly met the crisis by responding, "Yes, she left sometime ago and Sister Webster is here now!"

Randy and Dan hadn't seen each other for over a year. They bumped into each other after a football game.
Randy: "And how is your wife?"
Dan: "My wife has gone to heaven."
Randy: "Oh, I'm so sorry." Then realizing that wasn't the appropriate response, he countered by saying, "I guess I mean I'm glad." That didn't sound quite right either so he changed it, saying, "I mean I'm so surprised!"

EMPLOYEES

In the pay envelope of this employee was a note: "Your raise will become effective as soon as you do."

"Why did you leave your last job?" asked the manager.
    "Illness," said the job applicant.
    "What kind of illness?"
    "I don't know," the man said, "They just said they were sick of me."

Dennis to boss: "Sir, I've been with you for 25 years, and I've never before asked for a raise."
Boss: "That's why you've been with me for 25 years!"

"I've worked here for 8 years," an overworked employee said to her boss, "and I've been doing the work of 3 people. I want a raise."

"I can't give you a raise," the boss answered. "But if you'll tell me who the 2 people are, I'll fire them."

EMPLOYMENT

A young man applied for a job at a supermarket. The manager said, "Yes, I'll give you a job. Sweep out the store."

"But," said the young applicant, "I'm a college graduate."

The manager quietly replied, "Oh, that's all right. I'll show you how."

I could have been a parachutist, but nothing ever opened up.

I could have been a trapeze artist in the circus, but I just couldn't get the hang of it.

I could have been a professional bowler, but it simply wasn't up my alley.

I could have been an elevator operator, but I felt the job had too many ups and downs.

I could have been a librarian, but I shelved that idea.

Astronomer: My business is looking up.
Garbage Collector: Our business is picking up.

Tailor: My business is just sew, sew.

Egg Producer: Our business is not all that it's cracked up to be.

This notice was distributed to all the employees of the company:

> Due to the increased competition and a keen desire to remain in business, we find it necessary to institute a new policy.
>
> Effective immediately, we are asking that somewhere between starting time and quitting time—and without infringing too much on the time usually devoted to lunch periods, coffee breaks, rest periods, story telling, vacation planning, and rehashing of yesterday's TV programs—that each employee endeavor to find some time that can be set aside and known as the "work break."
>
> To some this may seem a radical innovation, but we honestly believe the idea has great possibilities.
>
> While the adoption of the "work break" plan is not compulsory, it is hoped that each employee will be interested enough to give the plan a fair trial.
>
> (Weaver Publishing Co.)

ENGLISHMEN

An Englishman heard an American say, "The happiest years of all my life, were spent in the arms of another man's wife—Lucy, my mother."

The Englishman thought that was worth repeating to a friend of his. His version was, "The happiest years of all of my life, were spent in the arms of another man's wife. Er, ah, by jove, I forget her name!"

This visitor from London overheard a fellow in Dublin, Ireland, tell his girl friend, "Darling, when I gaze into your face, time ceases."

He decided to duplicate those nice words when he got back to his girl friend in London. As he put his arm around her he whispered, "Darling, you have a face—a face that would stop a clock!"

An Englishman was taken to a New York hotel. He and the room clerk became friendly and began swapping jokes.

The room clerk said to the Englishman, "I have a riddle: My mother and my father had a baby. It wasn't my brother or my sister. Who was it?"

The visitor thought for a moment and said, "I don't know. Who was it?"

"It was me!" answered the clerk.

The Englishman returned home and decided to try the riddle on his friend. "My parents had a baby. It wasn't my brother or my sister. Who was it?"

His friend replied, "I don't know. Who was it?"

"The room clerk at a New York Hotel," answered the Englishman.

ENTHUSIASM

A Swedish brother came back to his home church after spending a week at a summer Bible conference. He was bubbling over with enthusiasm.

They asked him to lead in prayer and he quickly responded, "Oh, Lord, it was so inspiring at the conference. The fellowship with all the saints was so good. The music lifted us to heaven, and the preaching, Lord, was marvelous! In fact, Lord, you just should have been there *yourself!*"

EVANGELISTS

An evangelist in downtown Philadelphia needed to know where the post office was. So he asked a newsboy for information.

Boy: "Go this way two blocks and then turn to the right."

Evangelist: "You seem like a bright fellow. Do you know who I am?"

Boy: "Nope!"

Evangelist: "I'm the preacher who is holding a revival in the big tent. If you come tonight, I'll show you the way to heaven."

Boy: "Aw, go on! You don't even know the way to the post office!"

EVOLUTION

Said a monkey, while swinging his tail,
to the baby monks—male and female,
"From your offspring, my dears,
in a few million years,
may evolve a professor at Yale."

EXERCISE

Bob Hope once said, "Today my heart beat 103,369 times; my blood traveled 168 million miles; I breathed 23,400 times; I inhaled 438 cubic feet of air; I ate 3 pounds of food; I drank 2.9 pounds of liquid; I perspired 1.43 pints; I generated 450 tons of energy; I spoke 4,800 words; I moved 750 major muscles; and I exercised 7 million brain cells. Gee, I'm just all tired out!"

EXPERTS

A fellow had two parrots and he wanted to know which was the male and which was the female.

A man standing near said, "I am a bird expert, and I can tell you. If you will notice every time the birds eat worms, the male bird always eats the male worms and the female bird always eats the female worms."

"Well how do you know which is the male worm and which is the female worm?"

"Well, I don't know that. I'm just a *bird* expert."

FACES

Two fellows were walking down the street:
Jack: "Hey, that girl smiled at me."
Pete: "I'm not surprised. The first time I saw
   you I laughed out loud."

Well, well, well. He's all dressed up and no
face to go.

He has a face of a saint—a Saint Bernard.

I don't really recall your face, but your breath
smells familiar!

I never forget a face, but in your case I'm willing
to make an exception.

He should join the Ku Klux Klan. He'd look a
lot better with a hood over his face.

Rain makes flowers pretty I hear:
I wish it would rain on her for a year.

He has a "ski jump" nose.

Does your face hurt you?
It's killing me!

I know how homely I are,
I know that my face is no star,
But why should I mind it
for I am behind it;
The fellow in front gets the jar!

FARMERS

A farmer increased egg production by putting up this sign in his hen house: "An egg a day keeps Colonel Sanders away."

A gal from the city asked an old farmer, "Which is correct grammatically: to say a hen is 'setting' or 'sitting'?"

The farmer replied, "I guess I don't know that one, miss, and it really don't interest me none. What does interest me, when I hear a hen cackle, is if she's 'laying' or 'lying.'"

The farmer told his neighbor that he accidently left the milking machine on his best cow all night and she had given 21 gallons.
Neighbor: "How is she?"
Farmer: "She's proud, but pooped!"

FAREWELLS

At a farewell for a departing pastor a tearful parishioner said to him, "I don't know what we will do when you are gone, Pastor."

Minister: "Oh, don't be upset, the church will soon get a better man than I am."

Parishioner: "That's what they all say, but they keep getting worse and worse."

FATHERS

"What were your father's last words?"

"He didn't have any. Mother was with him to the end."

FEAR

A teen-ager was on the Sunday night program for a short speech. It was very evident that he was scared. In a shaky voice he said, "Folks, I'm sure this speech is going to be good; my knees are already applauding me."

FINANCES

Mike: We like this house, but the landlord asks too much for the rent.

Bud: Really?

Mike: Yes, last month he asked for it 4 different times.

In response to a request that he immediately pay a bill for $258, John Doe wrote the following:

My Dear Sir:

In reply to your request to send a check, I wish to inform you that the condition of my bank account makes it almost impossible. My shattered financial condition is due to federal laws, state laws, county laws, city laws, liquor laws, corporation laws, mother-in-laws, brother-in-laws, and outlaws.

I am compelled to pay a business tax, amusement tax, head tax, school tax, gas tax, light tax, sales tax, liquor tax, carpet tax, income tax, food tax, furniture tax, and excise tax. I am required to get a business license, car license, hunting and fishing license, truck license, not to mention the marriage license, and dog license.

I am expected to contribute to every society and organization which the genius of man is capable of bringing to life: to women's relief, the unemployment relief, and the gold diggers' relief. Also, to every hospital and charitable organization including the Red Cross, the Black Cross, the Purple Cross and the double cross.

I am required to carry life insurance, property insurance, liability insurance, burglar insurance, tornado insurance, flood insurance. In my business, I am inspected, expected, suspected, disrespected, rejected, examined, reexamined, informed, required, summoned, fined, and compelled.

Except for the miracle that happened, I could not enclose this check. The wolf that comes to many doors nowadays just had pups in my kitchen. I sold them and here is your money.

Yours faithfully,
John Doe

FISHING

After about an hour of fishing the little girl suddenly threw down her pole and cried, "I quit!"

Dad: "What's the matter?"

Girl: "Nothing except I can't seem to get waited on."

61

Sid and Bill had been out fishing, and the luck was good. A fine catch of bass lay in the boat.

"Let's come back here tomorrow," suggested Bill. "We won't find a better spot anywhere."

"That's OK with me," concurred Sid, "but how will we ever find this exact place again?"

Bill snorted. "Sid," he said, "you don't know enough to come out of the rain. I'll show you how." And he took a piece of chalk out of his pocket, and marked a big X on the side of the boat. "That'll do it," he said.

"But, Bill," objected Sid, scratching his head perplexedly, "how do we know that they'll rent us the same boat tomorrow?"

FLOWERS

Joe: "Hey, Jim, you are the flower of your family."

Jim: "What do you mean?"

Joe: "Well, you are either a budding genius or a blooming idiot."

A chrysanthemum by any other name would be a lot easier to spell.

FOOD

John is such a talented "do-it-yourself" man. Recently he built a beautiful bay window. He did it all with only two tools—a knife and a fork!

There was a young person named Ned
who dined before going to bed
on lobster and ham,
and pickles and jam,
and when he awoke he was dead.

He who indulges bulges!

Johnny was eating a hot fudge sundae and
enjoying it immensely. He was heard to say, "I
wish I had a neck like a giraffe, so I could
taste it for a week!"

Our backyard fireplace grill relieves
our summer mealtime tedium.
I charcoal broil our thick steaks rare,
my face and fingers medium.

It happened at a summer youth camp. As the
morning session came to a close many teens
came forward to consecrate their lives to the
Lord. The hymn, "Where He Leads Me, I Will
Follow," deeply touched their hearts.

Then they went to the dining hall for the
noon meal. It consisted of leftovers. Several
of them started griping about the food. One of
the counsellors stood up and said, "Hey kids,
I don't think you should sing, 'Where He Leads
Me, I Will Follow,' unless you are willing to
say, 'What he feeds me I will swallow!' "

Mary had a little lamb, a lobster, and some
   prunes;

A glass of milk, a piece of pie, and then some
    macaroons.
It made the waitresses all grin to see her
    order so.
And when they carried Mary out her face was
    white as snow.

It's not the *minutes* you spend at the table that
make you fat, it's the *seconds*.

Mother: "Now Joseph, you must eat your
    spinach. It will put color in your cheeks."
Joe: "Yes, but who wants green cheeks?"

Wife: "This is rabbit stew we're having tonight."
Husband: "I thought so. I just found a hair in
    mine."

Did you ever notice that people who don't count
their calories, usually have the figures to prove
it?

Boy at picnic: "This is sure a swell picnic.
I've only been here a half hour and I've got a
stomachache already!"

Shake and shake
The catsup bottle
None will come
And then a lot'll.
(Richard Armour)

FOOTBALL

Mildred: "What is your brother in college?"
Susan: "He's a halfback."
Mildred: "I mean in his studies."
Susan: "Oh, in his studies he's away back."

FRENCH

"Why are the Smith's taking French lessons?"
"They've adopted a French baby and they
want to understand what the little fellow says
when he learns to talk."

FRIEND

A true friend is one who thinks you're a good
egg even though you're half-cracked.

He's the kind of man who picks his friends—to
pieces.

Platonic friendship: The interval between the
introduction and the first kiss.

FUNERALS

A silly young man, Mr. Clyde,
at a funeral service was spied.
When asked, "Who is dead?"
he just giggled and said,
"I don't know. I just came for the ride."

A young minister was conducting the funeral service of one of his deacons. Pointing to the corpse he declared, "Friends, we have here only the shell. The nut has gone!"

Pastor: "This corpse has been a member of our church for over 30 years!"

Her singing was the kind that was appropriate to augment grief at funerals.

FUNERAL DIRECTORS

Old Ike Brown had been married twice and both wives had died and were buried in the family plot at the cemetery. Ike talked things over with the funeral director.

"I suppose one of these days you'll be burying me out there in the family plot, and I want to give you some instructions. My first wife was Milly. I loved her very much. My second wife was Tilly and I loved her as much as I loved Milly. Between the graves of Milly and Tilly is the space for me when I die. Now I want you to measure the distances between the graves very carefully. I want to be buried exactly the same distance from Milly as I am from Tilly. But, if you happen to make a little mistake in the measuring, then *tilt me a little toward Tilly.*"

After Mrs. Bonham's husband had been care-fully embalmed, the funeral director asked her if she was fully satisfied with everything. As she looked things over she said, "Oh, I'm so sorry you've used a brown suit on him. He never wore brown. Could you change it to a dark blue suit?"

"I think so," replied the funeral director. "We have another man here for burial who has a blue suit, and I think we can make the change."

A few hours later the widow returned and she was pleased to observe her husband now attired in a dark blue suit. She asked the funeral director, "Wasn't it quite difficult to switch suits?"

He explained, "Oh, we didn't switch suits. We simply changed heads!"

GIRLS

Eugenia: "I caught my boy friend flirting."
Jane: "Yes, that's the way I caught mine, too."

GOOD NEWS—BAD NEWS

The good news: Your son just broke the diving record for the triple somersault from the high board for his school.
The bad news: There was no water in the pool.

The good news: I spotted the first robin of spring.
The bad news: He spotted me first!

The good news: You've made the Olympic javelin team.
The bad news: Your job is to catch the javelin.

GOLF

The lament of Mr. Overweight: "My difficulty is that when I get close enough to the ball to hit it, I can't see it. And when I get far enough from the ball to see it, I can't hit it."

Vic: "My wife says if I don't give up golf she's going to leave me."
Garth: "That's tough luck, Vic."
Vic: "Yes, I'm really going to miss her."

GOSSIP

She belongs to the meddle class.

She has a keen sense of rumor.

She's the vacuum sweeper type—she just purrs and takes in the dirt.

GOVERNMENT

Poor old George Washington. He couldn't blame his troubles on the previous administration.

When I was a boy, I was told anybody could become president of our nation. Now I'm beginning to believe it!

The North Carolina mountaineers tell this fable:

Once there was a king and he hired him a prophet for to prophet him his weather. And one evening the king he aimed to go see his best girl, so he notioned to wear his best clothes. Before leaving the palace he asked his prophet was hit liable to come on a rain before sundown. And the prophet says: "No, king, hit ain't a-coming on, not even a sizzle-suzzle."

So the king he put on his best clothes and started on his way, and along come a farmer riding a jackass, and the farmer says: "King, if'n you ain't aiming to git them clothes wetted you'd best go back home, 'cause hit's a-coming on to rain a trash-mover and a gully-washer."

And the king says: "I hired me a high-wage prophet for to prophet me my weather, and he allows hit ain't a-coming on, not even a sizzle-suzzle."

So the king kept a-goin'—and hit came on—a trash-mover and a gully-washer. And the king's clothes was wetted and his best girl she seen him and laughed.

The king was all mad and he went back to his palace and he throwed out his high-wage prophet, and he says, "Fetch me that there farmer," and they fetched him. And the king says, "Farmer, I throwed out my high-wage prophet, and I aim to hire you to prophet me my weather from this onwards."

And the farmer says, "King, I ain't no prophet. All I done this evening was to look at my jackass, because if'n hit's a-coming on to rain his ears lops down, and the lower they lays the harder hit's a-coming on to rain, and this evening they was a-laying and a-lopping."

So the king says, "Go home, farmer, and I'll hire me that jackass."

And friends, that's how it started, and jackasses hev been holding all the high-wage gov'ment jobs ever since!

Next time a man tells you talk is cheap, ask him if he knows how much a session of Congress costs.

Congress is so strange. A man gets up to speak and says nothing. Nobody listens—and then everybody disagrees.

The boys are in such a mood that if someone introduced the Ten Commandments, they'd cut them down to eight. (Senator Norris Cotton)

GRAMMAR

If I'd a knowed that you'd a went, I would have came and sawed you off.

My grammar is excellent. I've only made one mistake in grammar in all my life, and I knowed it the minute I done it!

GRANDPARENTS

"Did I ever tell you about my grandchildren?" a proud grandfather asked his friend.

"No," replied the friend, "and you don't know how much I have appreciated it."

Grandpa Carlson to some of his friends: "My wife and I are enjoying our grandchildren so much. I told her this is so much fun, we should have had them first."

HAIR

Men wear their hair in 3 ways: parted, unparted, and departed.

HEALTH

Overheard during a healing service.
   "I'm surely aching from arthritis."
   "Glad to meet you, I'm Ollie Olson from Minneapolis."

The secret of good health is to eat raw onions, but the difficulty is how to keep it a secret.

Epitaph on a hypochondriac's tombstone,
"I told you I was sick."

HEAVY

He's afflicted with Dunlap's disease. His stomach *done laps* over.

HISTORY

Think of our ancestors. Are they behind us or did they go ahead of us? This is one of the mysteries of history.

America was founded by four fathers.

Anna: "Martha, did you ever study ancient history?"
Martha: "No, I always figured it was better to let by-gones be by-gones!"

HOME

The fellow that owns his own home is always just coming out of the hardware store.

Home is where the college student home for the holidays isn't. (Laurence J. Peter)

HONEYMOONS

It happened at Niagara Falls. Al met his friend, Scotty, while walking near the American Falls.
Al: "Hey, Scotty, good to see you. What are you doing here at Niagara Falls?"
Scotty: "I'm here on my honeymoon."
Al: "Well, congratulations! And where's your beautiful bride?"
Scotty: "I didn't bring her along. She's been here before!"

HOSPITALS

Sign in a hospital: Our prices are not as stiff as our patients.

HOUSEKEEPING

The room looked very "Christmessy."

HOW?

Two hillbillies were greeting each other.
Randy: "How are your hogs?"
Cy: "Oh, they're all right. How are your folks?"

HUMILITY

An evangelist had announced he would preach on "humility" the Thursday night of the campaign. At message time on Thursday he announced, "I was going to bring my sermon on humility tonight, but the crowd is much smaller than I expected, so I'll wait to preach it some other night."

Did you hear about the famous evangelist who authored a book on "humility"? It's publication was delayed because the printer ran out of I's.

HUMOR (from the mission fields)

Missionaries are notorious for making blunders in the new language they are learning. The nationals are usually very patient, plus very

74

amused. The following are some examples (mainly from South America):

The missionary should have said, *"Muy bien, todos pónganse de pie."* ("All right, everybody stand up.")
    Instead he said, *"Muy bien, todos pies arriba."* ("All right, everyone feet up!")

It was a solemn ordination service but the missionary in charge really goofed. Instead of saying *"Yo te ordeno"* ("I ordain you"), he mistakenly said, *"Yo te ordeño"* ("I milk you!").

In making the announcements for the week the missionary meant to say, "There are meetings *(reuniones)* for the women on Thursdays, and meetings *(reuniones)* for the men on Fridays."
    But what came out was, "There will be kidneys *(riñones)* for the women on Thursdays, and kidneys *(riñones)* for the men on Fridays."

The single missionary woman needed to buy a saltshaker *(salero)* at the store. But she asked the store manager if they had a *soltero* (single man) available!

Whenever visiting pastors preach on a mission field, the sermon is interpreted into the language of that country. In South America the interpreter for this visiting preacher was a national pastor who knew English quite well, but was not acquainted with some of the picturesque phrases of our language. The introduction went as follows:

Preacher: "I am delighted to be here." (The national pastor had no difficulty translating that.)

Preacher: "In fact, I am tickled to death to be here." That was a tough one to translate! The interpreter said, "Folks, our guest says that he has scratched himself until he died!"

A bachelor missionary was on a bus traveling from Quito to Riobamba in Ecuador. A single missionary woman was making the same trip. An Ecuadorean passenger asked the missionary if the woman was his wife. He meant to explain that she was a fellow missionary, but what came out was, "She is my *compañera no más.*" (She is *only my mistress!*)

Somewhat different, but still related to language difficulties is the story of an immigrant in New York City, riding on the subway. He was hanging onto a strap.

A woman passenger said, "There is room for you here if you'd like to be seated."

He replied, "Thanks so much, but I don't want to cockroach upon you."

She tried to be helpful saying, "I believe you mean you don't want to *encroach* upon me."

"Oh, that's right," he replied, "when it's a man it is *cock*roach, but when it's a woman it is *hen*roach."

In our early days in Ecuador I was invited to conduct an evangelistic campaign in the port city of Guayaquil, the first such opportunity of my missionary experience. It was glorious! There were over forty decisions for Christ.

The same week, however, my wife Wilda had an appendectomy in a Guayaquil hospital. I wrote a report back to our supporting church in Pontiac, Michigan. They published condensations of the missionary letters in the magazine *Gospel Echoes*. The condensation of my report read this way:

"I've just had the most enjoyable week of my entire ministry—Wilda was in the hospital for an appendicitis operation!" (Robert Savage)

The announcer was making a station break at the missionary radio station HCJB, Quito, Ecuador. "Here at HCJB we present programs in various languages: in English, Spanish, Swedish, and Rubbish!"

HUSBANDS

Being a husband is like any other job. It helps a lot if you like the boss.

Art: In my house, I make all the major decisions and my wife makes the minor ones. For example, I decide such things as the Middle East crisis, corruption in government, the OPEC policy, and nuclear disarmament. My wife decides minor things like where we will go on vacation, what house to buy, when to get a new car, and what kind of furniture to purchase.

He had been away from home on a business trip for 2 weeks. He went into a restaurant and when the waitress came for his order, he said, "Bring me two slices of burnt toast, a cup of cold coffee; then sit down and nag me. I'm just plain lonesome."

A man was asked who was boss in his home. He replied, "Well, my wife bosses the children; the children boss the dog and cat, and I—well, I just say anything I like to the geraniums."

It was a Sunday afternoon and John had been watching football on TV, one game after another. Finally he fell asleep in the chair and slept there all night.

When his wife arose in the morning, she was afraid he'd be late for work. "Get up dear," she said. "It's twenty to seven!"

In an instant he was awake. "In whose favor?" he shouted.

Two men were talking about their wives.

Larry: "We had a tough quarrel yesterday but finally she came crawling to me on her hands and knees."

Ned: "What did she say?".

Larry: "She said, 'Larry, you come out from under that bed and fight like a man!'"

There were two lines being formed by scores of husbands. One line had a sign, "Henpecked Husbands," and the line was long. The other line had a sign, "Husbands Who Are Not Henpecked," and there was only one fellow in it. He was asked, "Are you sure you are in the right line?" He answered, "Er . . . ah, . . . yes, because this is where my wife *told* me I should be!"

Joe: "I've got to rush home and explain to my wife."
Tom: "Explain what?"
Joe: "I don't know; I'm not home yet."

She: "Darling, the man next door kisses his wife everytime he sees her. Why don't you do that?"
He: "I would, but I don't know her well enough yet."

He: "I sure wish you could bake bread like my mother used to."
She: "And I sure wish you would make dough like my dad used to!"

Pete: "It has been tough. My wife has been nursing a grouch all week."
Tom: "What's the matter, you been sick?"

Wife to sleepy husband: "Charlie, wake up! It's garbage day!"
Husband: "Just tell him we don't want any today."

About 4 A.M. she let out an awful scream that could be heard a block away. Henry woke up with a start and asked, "What is the matter with you, screaming like that?"

She gasped, "I've just had an awful dream: I dreamed I was at an auction sale of husbands. Some husbands sold for $500, others for $5,000, and some even went for $10,000."

Henry's head was already swelling a bit as he inquired, "Yes, and what did husbands like *me* sell for?"

"Oh, Henry, that's why I screamed! They had husbands like you wrapped up like green onions and were selling them two bunches for 50¢!"

Minister: "If there is anyone here who knows of a truly perfect person, please stand up."

After a long pause a meek looking fellow in the back stood. "Do you really know a perfect person?" he was asked.

"Yes, sir, I do," answered the little man.

"Would you please tell the congregation who this rare, perfect person is?" pursued the preacher.

"Yes, sir, my wife's first husband."

Al: "They tell me your wife is outspoken."
Herb: "By whom?"

As he was preparing to go to the store his wife told him to get a head of cabbage.

"What size?" he asked.

"Oh, about the size of your head," she told him.

On the way he met a friend who had a garden. "Just go over to my garden and take any head of cabbage you want," the friend offered generously.

Later, another friend asked the gardener, "What kind of idiot did you have in your garden? When I went by, he was trying his hat on one head of cabbage after another!"

Two husbands were bringing each other up to date on getting along with their wives. Nate said to Roy, "What are you anyhow, a man or a mouse?"

"I'm a man," Roy responded.

"What makes you think so?" queried Nate.

"Because," Roy retorted, "my wife is afraid of a mouse!"

(See also: Dads, Fathers, Marriage, Weddings, Wives)

HYPOCRITES

Preacher: "How come I never see you in church anymore, Morris?"

Morris: "There are too many hypocrites there, Reverend."

Preacher: "Don't worry, fellow; there's always room for one more."

INDIANS

Watching a western show on television, a farm boy asked his father, "Was the white man really smarter than the Indian?"

The father answered: "Son, when the Indians ran the country, they didn't have to pay any taxes, they didn't accumulate any debts, and the women did all the work. No one can improve on that."

INHERITANCE

The man who owned the city's newspaper had 3 sons. He offered ownership of the paper to the son who could write the most sensational headline of only three words.

The first son's headline was, "Reagan Turns Communist."

The second son concocted this: "Khomeini Becomes Christian."

But the third son inherited the newspaper when his headline was submitted. It had only two words, "Pope Elopes."

INFERIORITY COMPLEX

When the psychologist asked him what his problem was, the patient replied, "I'm suffering from an inferiority complex."

The doctor prescribed a complicated series of tests. After several weeks the results of the tests were tabulated and the appropriate correlations made.

When the patient had his next appointment, the doctor informed him. "I have some interesting news for you."

"What's that?" asked the patient.

"It isn't a complex," answered the psychologist, "You *are* inferior."

INTRODUCTIONS

The toastmaster introduced the speaker saying, "We are delighted to have with us this evening Roger Peterson. Mr. Peterson is from California where he has a very successful oil business with a reported profit last year of $100,000."

In reply the speaker said he would have to clarify a few items. "I'm really not from California—I'm from Pittsburgh. It's not the oil business—my business is steel. The figure wasn't $100,000—it was $50,000. And it wasn't a profit—it was a loss!"

Toastmaster. "Dr. Savage is a great wit. He had two sons and passed it on to them—half to each one!"

Toastmaster: "It is our privilege to have with us this evening Stanley H. Anderson. I asked what the initial 'H' stands for, and was informed it stands for 'Haystack.' When he was born his father looked at him and gave him the middle name of 'Haystack' saying, 'This is the last straw!' "

Toastmaster introducing the banquet speaker: "I could listen to this wonderful music for an hour more, but unfortunately we have a speaker."

After a particularly eloquent introduction the speaker at the banquet greeted those assembled by observing, 'An introduction like this is like flattery. And flattery is like perfume—it is to be sniffed, but not swallowed."

JEWS

A Catholic priest and a Jewish rabbi were sitting together at a banquet.

Priest: "Tell me, when are you going to break down and eat a little ham?"

Rabbi: "At your wedding!"

LAWYERS

Sign over door of a divorce lawyer: "Satisfaction Guaranteed—or Your Honey Back."

LAZINESS

Merle: "I always do my hardest work before breakfast."

Mike: "What's that?"

Merle: "Getting out of bed."

Jack (trying to open his eyes as the alarm clock rings at 7 A.M.): "I'd sure enjoy mornings a lot better if they came later in the day."

Old Zeke: "Praise the blessed Lord for the nights in which to sleep and the days in which to *rest.*"

LETTERS

Mr. and Mrs. Powell received this letter from Linda, their daughter, a sophomore at college.

Dear Mom and Dad:

Everything is OK, well, almost everything. You see, I have had a terrible headache ever since I jumped from my dormitory during a fire. A fine-looking young man was passing my window when he saw the flames leaping from the window. He was kind enough to call the fire department and ambulance. Since my furniture was burned up and my room destroyed, I have been staying with him at his apartment. I have thought seriously about marrying him, but I know how you feel about mixed marriages.

Mom and Dad, relax. None of the above happened to me. I don't have a headache, there was no fire in the dorm, and I am not living with a young man. But I am writing to tell you I just received my report card. I have three D's and two F's. I just thought if I put this in a different perspective it wouldn't upset you so much.

Your loving daughter,
Linda

LIMERICKS

There was a young fellow named Hall,
who fell in the spring in the fall.
'Twould have been a sad thing
if he died in the spring.
but he didn't—he died in the fall.

I sat next to a duchess at tea.
'Twas just as I thought it would be,
Her rumblings abdominal, were simply
    phenomenal,
and everyone thought it was me.

An electrical student named Weir
possessed not an atom of fear.
He had a desire to grab a live wire. (Pause)
Most any last line will do here.

A flea and a fly (in a flue) were imprisoned.
So what could they do?
"Let us flee," said the fly.
"Let us fly," said the flea.
So they flew through the flaw in the flue.

There was a young man from Peru,
who dreamed he was eating a shoe.
He woke up that night
with a terrible fright,
and found it was perfectly true.

A cheerful old bear at the zoo
could always find something to do.
When it bored him you know
to walk to and fro,
he reversed it and walked fro and to!

LOST

Little Timmy got lost. He looked up and down
the street in vain. Finally he went up to a
policeman on the corner. "Mister," he said
plaintively, "did you see a lady go by without
me?"

LOYALTY

"There isn't anything in the world that I
wouldn't do for Eddie, and there isn't anything
he wouldn't do for me. That's why we have
gone through life not doing anything for each
other."

MALAPROPISMS

"We sold our house and are moving into one of those pandemoniums."

"That politician is nothing but a sneak in the grass."

"I resent insinuendoes."
(Mayor Richard J. Daley)

"She picked a lawyer out of the phone book at ransom."

"We shall reach greater and greater platitudes of achievement." (Mayor Richard J. Daley)

MARRIAGE

Two can live as cheaply as one . . . for half as long.

I loved her then—I love her now—I love her now and then.

The marriage of Adam and Eve was ideal for two reasons: First, Adam didn't have to hear about all the men she could have married, and second, Eve didn't have to hear about the wonderful way his mother cooked meals.

Two can live just as cheaply as one . . . and generally they have to.

A 7-year-old had never seen his grandmother. She came to visit and he was quite impressed as he looked her over.

"Are you really my grandmother?" he asked.

"Yes, Jimmy, I'm your grandmother on your father's side."

"Well, if that's the case, Grandma, I'm telling you right now, you're on the losing side."

A mother had a son and a daughter, who were both married. The mother told her friend: "My daughter was fortunate! She married a fellow who is so helpful. He frequently washes the dishes. He helps with their baby and even cooks some of the meals.

"But my poor son! He really got a bad deal! Why that woman he married is so unjust. Believe it or not, she expects my son to *wash dishes, help with their baby,* and even wants him to prepare *some of the meals!* My heart really goes out to him!"

Jane: "I could have married anybody I pleased."
Ellen: "Then why are you single?"
Jane: "I never pleased anyone."

A woman was telling how she had been married four times—first to a banker, then to an actor, next to a preacher and finally to an undertaker. "You know how it is," she explained, "One for the money, 2 for the show, 3 to get ready, and 4 to go!"

A certain young fellow named Beebee
wished to marry a lady named Phoebe.
"But," he said, "I must see
what the clerical fee be
before Phoebe be Phoebe Beebee."

Al: "Are you married?"
Jim: "Yes, my wife's an angel. Are you married?"
Al: "Yes, but mine's still living."

They married for better or worse. He couldn't do better and she couldn't do worse.

A marriage counselor was asking a woman some questions about her disposition.

"Did you wake up grumpy this morning?" the counselor inquired.

"No," replied the woman, "I just let him sleep."

A friend remarked to a man whose marriage seemed very happy, "My, how wonderfully you and your wife get along. Don't you ever have any differences of opinion?"

"Oh, yes," was the reply, "we have quite a few."

"You must get over them quickly."
"Ah, that's the secret," said the husband."
I never tell her about them."

Wife: "You're not as gallant as when I was
    a gal."
Husband: "You're not as buoyant as when I
    was a boy."

(See also: Weddings, Husbands, Wives)

MATHEMATICS

In algebra you use X when you don't know what
you are talking about.

MEMORIAL

In a midwestern state, a newspaper reported
that a widower had donated a loudspeaker to
his church in memory of his wife!

MEMORY

I remember your name perfectly, but I just
can't think of your face!

Jim: "Great Scot! I can't for the life of me
    remember who wrote *Ivanhoe.*"
Mike: "And I can't recall who the dickens
    wrote *The Tale of Two Cities.*"

Just a line to say I'm living,
    that I'm not among the dead,

though I'm getting more forgetful
    and more mixed up in my head.

For sometimes I cannot remember,
    when I start to climb the stairs,
if I'm going up for something
    or have just come down from there.

And before the fridge so often
    my poor mind is filled with doubt.
Have I just put food away, or
    have I come to take it out?

Oft-times when it's dark outside,
    and with my nightcap on my head,
I don't know if I'm retiring
    or just getting out of bed.

So remember I do love you,
    and I wish that you were here.
And I see it's nearly mail time;
    I must say, "Good-bye, my dear."

P.S.
There I stood beside the mailbox
    with my face so very red,
instead of mailing you this letter
    I have opened it instead.

METRIC SYSTEM

When we change to the metric system, many of
our old sayings and proverbs will have to be
brought up to date using meters, grams, liters,
instead of miles, pounds, pints, etc.

Examples:

A miss is as good as 1.6 kilometers.

Put your best 0.3 of a meter forward.

Spare the 5.03 meters and spoil the child.

Twenty-eight grams of prevention is worth 453 grams of cure.

Give a man 2.5 centimeters and he'll take 1.6 kilometers.

Peter Piper picked 8.8 liters of pickled peppers.

MINDS

When a fellow ain't got much mind, it don't take him long to make it up. (Will Rogers)

He knew his own mind well, and it was no place he would like to be cooped up in for very long.

MISSIONARIES

(See: Humor from the mission fields)

MONEY

A TV listener to a Billy Graham special sent a check for $50, but she didn't sign it—she wanted it to be an anonymous gift!

Isn't it crazy? Nowadays if someone says he is paying in cash, you get suspicious. You wonder if his credit is good!

It's true that money talks, but in these days a dollar doesn't have enough cents to say anything worthwhile.

One reason why it's so hard to save money is that our neighbors are always buying something we can't afford.

If you want to get rid of a pesty acquaintance just lend him some money.

A boy came home from Sunday school and began emptying his pockets of pennies, dimes and nickles.
Dad: "Where did you get that money, Jerry?"
Boy: "At church they have two plates full of it!"

MORONS

A moron by the name of Rocky got a job as a delivery boy for a pet shop. One day his job was to deliver a rabbit to: Mrs. Grant, 1563 Sunset Blvd.

He put the name and address in his pocket, jumped into the pickup truck and was on his way. Every few minutes he pulled out the slip of paper to refresh his memory. "I know where I'm going—Mrs. Grant, 1563 Sunset Blvd."

But suddenly the truck hit a deep pothole, and he careened off the road into a ditch. The rabbit escaped and began to run for its life across the open field.

Rocky watched the pet and started laughing. A passer-by asked him what was so funny. Rocky answered, "Did you see that crazy rabbit running across the field? He doesn't know where he's going because I've got the name and address right here in my pocket."

The visitor watched the moron at the typewriter, and inquired, "What are you doing?"

Moron: "I'm writing a letter."

Visitor: "To whom?"

Moron: "It's to me."

Visitor: "What does it say?"

Moron: "How do I know? I won't get it until tomorrow."

(See also: So Dumb)

MOTHERS

She is "infanticipating."

Mother: Every time you're naughty, I get another gray hair.

Son: Gee, Mom, you must have been a holy terror when you were young. Just look at Grandma!

MOTHERS-IN-LAW

Andy went to his boss saying, "I wonder if I could get the afternoon off. I'd like to attend my mother-in-law's funeral." The boss granted his request.

That afternoon the boss went to a ball game at Wrigley Field to watch the Cubs play. To his amazement Andy was there too. "I thought you said you wanted to attend your mother-in-law's funeral," remonstrated the boss.

"Yes, I sure would," answered Andy, "but she is still very much alive."

As his dear wife lay dying she whispered to Willard, her husband. "Darling, at my funeral I want to ask that you ride in the same car with my mother."

"OK, I will," he answered, "but it will sure ruin the day for me."

One of the outstanding families of Quito, Ecuador, decided to spend a vacation period in the jungle area. When they returned Sr. Andrade was giving a report to his friend, Sr. Lopez.

Lopez: "How did things go?"

Andrade: "Sort of good and sort of bad."

Lopez: "What do you mean?"

Andrade: "One day we were taking a walk and a tiger leaped out from the jungle to attack my wife."

Lopez: "What did you do?"

Andrade: "I took my revolver and shot him dead."

Lopez: "Nice work! Congratulations!"

Andrade: "But that isn't all. Another time we were taking a little stroll and a rhinoceros burst forth wanting to attack my son."

Lopez: "What did you do?"

Andrade: "I whipped out my revolver and shot him dead."

Lopez: "That's great! Congratulations!"

Andrade: "But that isn't all. Another day we were walking down a trail and a lion jumped out to attack my mother-in-law!"

Lopez: "What did you do? What did you do?"

Andrade: "I walked up to that lion and I said,
'*Buen provecho.*' Have a good meal!"

MOUTHS

It is usually the fellow with the big mouth who
bites off more than he can chew.

MUSIC

Two editors of a music publishing house were
examining manuscripts of new songs sent to
them. One of them observed, "I've never seen a
song with such corny lyrics, such silly senti-
mentality, such a repetitive melody. Hey, it sure
looks like we've got one that will be a top hit!"

The soloist was singing in a high-soprano voice.
She came to the phrase, "He's the fairest of
10,000," and her voice broke as she came to
the "10." Undaunted, she tried again, but met
with no greater success the second time.

"Give me my note again," she requested of
the pianist, and made a frantic third attempt.

"Lady," someone in the audience called, "I
don't think you're gonna make it. Don't you
think you'd better try for 5,000 this time?"

The tenor soloist was delighted when one of
the parishioners spoke to him after the church
service. "You have a very mellow voice," he
said.

The soloist got out his dictionary when he
arrived at home. The definition he found for
"mellow" was "over-ripe and almost rotten."

Mel to his wife: "Does my practicing on my trombone make you nervous?"

Ruth: "It used to when I heard the neighbors discussing it, but now I just don't care what happens to you."

Jake: "I should have been a songwriter; I have a squeaking shoe."

Joan: "What has a squeaking shoe got to do with being a songwriter?"

Jake: "I've got music in my *sole!*"

I like music. I took music lessons at Sing-Sing, but I was usually somewhat behind the bars. My favorite song was: "Steal Away."

Show me a squirrel's home, and I'll show you a nutcracker's suite.

NATIONALITIES

Scotsman—Keeps the Sabbath . . . and everything else he can lay his hands on.

Irishman—Doesn't know what he wants . . . and isn't happy until he gets it.

Swede—Prays on Sunday . . . and on everyone else the rest of the week.

Englishman—A self-made man . . . and very proud of his maker.

Hollander—Can buy from a Jew, sell to a Scotsman . . . and still make a profit.

NORTH/SOUTH

It was a suicide attempt. He was about to jump from the window of the eighth floor. A man from the deep South saw him and tried to talk him out of it.

"For the sake of your mother, don't do it!" he pleaded.

"I don't have a mother," the would-be suicide answered.

"Well, think of your father."

"I don't have a father."

"Then consider how your wife will feel."

"I never married," the dejected fellow said.

"Well then, think of Robert E. Lee!" urged the Southerner.

"Robert E. Lee! Who's he?"

"Never mind, Yankee. Go ahead and jump."

NONSENSE

When they operated on father they opened mother's mail.

Life is just a bowl of cherries, and I guess I'm the pits.

A fellow was found with a rope around his wrist, strung from a light fixture. His buddy cut him down and said, "What in the world are you doing?"

"Committing suicide!"

"Well, you should have put it around your neck if you really wanted to commit suicide."

The fellow answered, "I tried it around my neck but it was choking me."

This is a battle of wits, and I came only half-armed.

Lloyd: "I'm a little stiff from bowling."
Clyde: "I got your name, but where did you say you are from?"

101

NURSES

Show me a man getting an injection from a cheerful nurse, and I'll show you a man taking a friendly needling.

OFFERINGS

For all preachers needing to raise money a unique plan has been developed.

First you have to obtain 50 female pigs. Next you will need 50 male deer. Then you put them all together in a corral and you'll discover you now have 100 *sows* and *bucks!*

When it comes to giving, some people stop at nothing.

One of the town's alcoholics got gloriously saved. Shortly afterward he went to a gospel service and put his last 25¢ in the offering. The result was he had no bus fare and had to walk home.

The bartender heard about it and ridiculed him, "You're such a dumb fool, you give your last quarter to the church and have to walk home."

The new Christian answered, "Not half as much a fool as I used to be when I'd give you my last 25¢ and then wouldn't be able to walk home."

It was a conversation between a pig and a chicken. Each one claimed a greater degree of consecration than the other to the gospel cause. They came to a church and read a sign, "Annual breakfast next Saturday. Ham and eggs will be served." The pig, realizing the implications, said, "You see what I mean, you hens give out of your abundance, but for us it's a real sacrifice!"

The most frustrated feeling I've ever had was to be caught in church with nothing smaller than a $20 bill.

He dropped a quarter in the plate,
then meekly raised his eyes;
Glad that his weekly rent was paid
to mansions in the skies.

When the church offering was received a fine Christian young man, who had saved $25 as a start to go to Bible college, put the whole amount in the plate. A very wealthy man in contrast put 25¢ in the plate. However, on the following day the young man received a surprise check for $250 in the mail, and the wealthy man received a letter from his mother-in-law that she was going to come and stay with them for two months!

One fellow put it this way: "I'm not going to be stingy and only give one tenth. I've decided I'm going to give a twentieth!"

OLD AGE

A man who says he is doing as much at 60 as he did at 20, wasn't doing much at 20.

An oldster was celebrating his 100th birthday. He was asked if he wanted to make any appropriate comments on this auspicious occasion. "If I had known I was going to live this long," he observed, "I would have taken better care of myself."

An oldster was telling of the difficulties he was experiencing. "I can't see like I used to see, and I can't hear like I used to hear, and by gorry, now I'm beginning to *smell bad.*"

The censustaker insisted that the 2 elderly women tell their age, but they stubbornly refused.
Censustaker: "We've got to put down some age for you."
Miss Stubborn: "OK then, put down the same age for us as you put down for the folks next door."
   The neighbors' name was Hill. So the censustaker wrote down, "As old as the Hills."

Three elderly ladies who were hard of hearing were riding on a bus together. A couple of windows were open and one of them said to another, "Windy, isn't it?"
   "No, it isn't Wednesday, it's Thursday," was the reply.

The third lady was listening in and added, "Yes, I'm thirsty, too! Let's get off and have a Coke."

(See also: Age, Birthdays)

OPTIMISTS

Nothing is *all* wrong. Even a clock that has stopped running is right twice a day.

OPTIMIST/PESSIMIST

Two fellows were employed by the same shoe company—one an optimist, the other a pessimist. They were assigned 2 different islands out in the Pacific.

After 2 weeks the pessimist sent a telegram to headquarters. "Returning home. Nobody wears shoes here."

About the same time the optimist sent his telegram, "Nobody has shoes here. Will need additional salesmen."

PATIENCE

A century ago if a fellow missed catching a stagecoach it didn't upset him. After all there would be another one in about a week. But today with all our hurry and worry, flurry and scurry, it we miss one section of a revolving door we have a conniption.

PEOPLE

I love mankind. It's people I can't stand.

PERSEVERANCE

Eight-year-old Frankie had been pestering his dad for a watch. After the seventeenth time, his father finally said, "Frankie, I don't want to hear any more about your wanting a watch."

At dinner that night each member of the family gave a Scripture verse. When it was Frankie's turn he said, "My verse is Mark 13:37: 'And what I say unto you, I say unto all, *Watch.*'"

POLITICIANS/POLITICS

A surgeon, an engineer, and a politician were talking together about the relative importance of their professions and which was the oldest.

Surgeon: "Look, it was a surgical operation when a rib was taken out of Adam to make Eve. So mine is the oldest profession."

Engineer: "Oh no, don't you remember that there was chaos everywhere, and the 6 days of creation gave us what we have now— order instead of that chaos. That was an engineer's job. Mine is the oldest profession."

Politician: "You are both wrong! Who produced the chaos? That belonged to my profession!"

Politics has got so expensive that it takes a lot of money even to get beat with. (Will Rogers)

A statesman is any politician it's considered safe to name a school after.

A political war is one in which everyone shoots from the lip.

POPULARITY

The professor got the impression that Mary was disliked by the other girls. He asked one of them why it was. "Why it's because she won last year's popularity contest."

PRAYER

A little boy prayed: "Lord, if you can't make me a better boy, don't worry about it. I'm having a real good time as it is."

A 4-year-old boy decided that he'd make an attempt at reciting the prayer which he had heard in church. "And forgive our trash-baskets," he asked, "as we forgive those who trashbasket against us."

A Christian farmer was in town at noon and went into a restaurant for a hamburger and french fries. When he was served, he quietly bowed his head to give the Lord thanks for his food.

Some fellows at the next table saw him and thought they would poke fun at him. One of them called out, "Hey, farmer, does everyone do that where you live?"

"No, son," answered the farmer, "the pigs don't."

Five-year-old Kathie had a habit of making long, drawn-out bedtime prayers. One evening her mother tried to shorten them and said "Amen" during a slight pause, but Kathie prayed on.

At another pause the mother suggested "Amen" once again.

Immediately Kathie said, "Dear God, don't pay any attention to her, she doesn't know when I'm done." (Freda B. Elliott)

When little Peter heard the minister shout as he prayed, he said to his mother, "Don't you think that if he lived nearer to God he wouldn't have to talk so loud?"

Two Senators were conversing in the anteroom of the U.S. Capitol. They were discussing who was the better Christian. One said, "Humph, I bet you $10 you can't even recite the Lord's Prayer."

"I bet you I can," replied the other.

"Well, let's hear you," the first challenged.

The other immediately intoned, "Now I lay me down to sleep, I pray thee, Lord, my soul to keep. . . ."

The first Senator listened with amazement. "Here's your $10," he said. "I sure didn't think you knew it!"

PREACHERS

Pastor Webster had a reputation for always limiting his sermons to exactly 25 minutes. But on this particular Sunday (to the dismay of all the congregation) he continued on and on for 55 minutes. Afterwards some of the parishioners asked him what happened.

He explained, "My custom is to place a cough drop in my mouth when I start to preach and it always dissolves in 25 minutes and so I know when to stop. But today, I made a mistake and instead of putting a cough drop in my mouth I put a button in there!"

Three pastors were having a little fellowship. One suggested: "Men, let's just be frank with each other and each one tell what his weakness is—his secret sin." They agreed.

No. 1: "I'll confess to you fellows that when the offering plates are placed on my office desk that, if no one is around, I simply can't resist the temptation to take a $10 bill from the plate and slip it into my pocket."

No. 2: "Well, since we are telling it like it is, I'll confess that my weak point is liquor. I have a bottle hidden in the bottom drawer of my desk and every once in a while, if no one is around, I take a swig."

No. 3: "Men, I might as well tell you that my weakness is . . . gossip. And I can hardly wait to get out of here!"

Pastor: "I don't mind if they look at their watches while I'm preaching to see what time it is, but it gets me very upset when they put them up to their ears to see if they are running or not."

He had chosen as his subject that Sunday morning, "The Immortality of the Soul." Waxing eloquent he came to the climax of his sermon:

"Behold the mountains, how they reach up toward the eternal heavens. Their grandeur, vastness, beauty and might o'erwhelms us. Some day, after millions and millions of years, these mountains will have all crumpled to dust but I never will. Behold the great oceans in their immensity, vastness, power and great depths. Yet

111

someday, after millions and millions of years, even the oceans will have dried up—but *I* never will!"

A lady came to the minister after he had given a sermon on hell. "Pastor," said she, "I never knew what hell really was like until you came here!"

Three girls were talking about the kind of man they wanted to marry.

Wilma: "I want to marry a food-market owner so I can get our food for nothing."

Jan: "I want to marry a dress-shop owner so I can be well dressed for nothing."

Ellen: "I want to marry a preacher so I can be good for nothing."

Two boys from the Dutch Reformed church decided to play a prank on their minister, the "dominie." One Saturday they slipped into the church and pasted together a few pages of the pulpit Bible. The next morning the "dominie" was reading from Genesis 2:22: "And the rib, which the Lord God had taken from man, made he a woman. . . ." At that point he had to turn the page and continuing in his rich, Dutch brogue he read, "fifty cubits broad and thirty cubits high."

The pastor looked puzzled but he maintained his composure saying, "Bless my soul, if this doesn't prove once again that most wonderful passage that we are 'fearfully and wonderfully made.' "

The visiting speaker was very short and had a high, squeaky voice. When he came to the pulpit his head could just barely be seen above the pulpit. He began saying, "Friends, my text for this morning is, 'Be not afraid, it is I.'"

Some in the congregation couldn't keep from snickering, so in anticipation of the evening service, the visitor went to the church in the afternoon and got several hymnbooks to fix a small platform behind the pulpit.

When he got up to preach, he stood on the hymnals and announced: "Friends, my text for this evening is, 'Yet a little while and ye see me no longer.'" Just at that time the hymnbooks fell over and down went the preacher.

He had been speaking for about an hour and it was very boring. A fellow in the balcony decided to heckle him and called out, "Louder! Louder!" After a couple of minutes he repeated his harassment yelling, "Louder! Louder!"

A cultured Englishman was sitting in the second row. At this point he stood up in a dignified way and directed himself to the disturber in the balcony. "Cawn't you hear?"

"No!" answered the annoyer.

The Englishman called, "Well then, old boy, thank the good Lord . . . and do sit down!"

One thing that bugged him about a pastor's responsibilities was being asked to speak at meetings of the Women's Auxiliary. He would do anything possible to avoid it.

In September the ladies were planning their

programs for a year ahead. The program chairman came to the pastor in the fall saying, "Pastor, could you be our speaker at the May meeting—Tuesday, the 16th?"

He got out his date book and said, "Oh, I'm so sorry I can't make it. I have a funeral scheduled for that date."

Minister: "I hope you won't charge too much to fix my car. I'm a poor preacher."
Mechanic: "Yes, I know. I heard you last Sunday."

The visiting preacher was shaking hands with folks in the foyer following his sermon. One of the congregation who was somewhat below par mentally said to him, "Sir, your sermon was too long . . . and you spoke too loud. Also, you didn't say anything worthwhile."

The chairman of the deacons overheard what was said and later attempted to apologize for what happened. "I'm so sorry for what Tommy said, but you really shouldn't pay any attention to it, because he really doesn't have the capacity to think things through for himself. He's only able to repeat what he's heard others say!"

Conversation between two preachers:
Pastor Woods: "Man, I feel lousy today!"
Pastor Harris: "Well I bet I feel worse than you do. My head is splitting."
Pastor Woods: "I just feel like I have a hole in my head."

Pastor Harris: "Well I feel like I have *two holes* in my head."

Pastor Woods: "You know that's what I don't like about you. You're always a 'holier than thou' type."

A famous clergyman told his congregation: "Every blade of grass is a sermon."

A few days later a parishioner saw him mowing his lawn and greeted him saying, "That's right, pastor—cut your sermons short!"

One Saturday night this pastor did a little back-sliding. He spent a couple of hours playing poker in a back room with three cronies. Sunday morning when he got up to preach he spied one of his poker friends in the congregation. With a solemn voice he intoned, "I want to mention an important verse which reads, 'He that knoweth a thing, and openeth not his mouth, him will I reward in secret,' Hezekiah 3:19."

It was a banquet of celebrities in New York City. The toastmaster discovered there was no clergyman present to bless the food. So he asked a lawyer to say grace. The lawyer stood up and began: "There being no clergyman present let us thank God."

For an hour and a half the preacher continued on and on with his sermon. Finally he asked: "What more can I say?" There was a brief pause. Then from the back of the church a voice was heard: "Well you might say, 'Amen.'"

A minister was hospitalized and the nurse accidentally placed a barometer instead of a thermometer in the minister's mouth to get his temperature. The reading was, "very dry and windy."

A young preacher who had been trained to preach without the use of notes began his sermon, "My text this morning is the passage from Revelation, 'Behold, I come quickly.'" But he couldn't think of the first point.

So he repeated, "Once again, My text this morning is, 'Behold I come quickly.'" And he said it with great emphasis and pounded the pulpit, but still the first point did not come to him. The third time he increased his volume still more with several pounds on the pulpit, "I repeat, my text for this morning is, 'Behold, I come quickly.'" Suddenly the pulpit toppled off the platform and the young man with it. He landed in the lap of a young lady in the front row. After great embarrassment he got back up on the platform and said to the young lady, "I certainly want to apologize for this very unfortunate incident."

"Oh, that's all right," she replied, "I should have known you were coming. You warned me 3 times in advance!"

A minister was scheduled to preach that night at a country church. About 5:30 P.M. the farmer's wife invited him to sit down at the table for a light meal.

"No thanks," he replied, "I find that if I eat just before I preach I don't do as well as if I wait until afterward to eat."

The farmer did not go to the meeting, staying at home. Afterwards he asked his wife, "How was the sermon?"

Her answer was, "He might just as well have et!"

Did you hear about the preacher who tape-recorded his sermon? When he sat down to listen to it, do you know what happened? He fell asleep!

In the foyer after the morning service 2 parishioners were commenting about the preacher. One observed, "He speaks very well, if he just had something to say!"

Dr. H. C. Morrison was a renowned Methodist preacher. In his early ministry after the church service, he asked a parishioner, "Did I preach too long?"

"No," the man answered, "you didn't preach too long, but you talked too much after you stopped preaching."

As the guest preacher began his sermon he had this word of explanation: "As I understand it, my job is to preach, and your job is to listen. If you finish before I do, please let me know."

A supply pastor was thumbing through the pulpit Bible when he came upon some sermon notes of the pastor. He scanned them a little and noticed this notation on the margin of one of the pages: "Yell like the dickens here—the argument's weak!"

Unlike many such stories this one is true. A pastor went deer hunting with 2 men of his church. A buck came along and the pastor pulled the trigger. The deer ran 100 yards or so and then collapsed—dead. But when they examined the deer's body they were unable to find any evidence of a bullet wound. How was that fine buck killed?

Finally they discovered what happened. The pastor's bullet had hit the deer in one ear and then had come out through the other. The two laymen were quick to observe, "That's the way it is with you, Pastor. What you send our way goes in one ear and comes out the other!"

This took place in the horse and buggy days. A pastor received a call to another church. He loaded his belongings on a horse-drawn wagon. The last two things to be loaded were a cow and his barrel of sermon notes.

When they reached their destination the pastor was horrified to discover that the cow had eaten all the sermon notes from the barrel. And do you know what happened to the cow? She went dry!

Pastor Murdock was visiting some of the families who hadn't attended church for some time. After repeated knocks on the door of the Turner family, the 10-year-old daughter opened the door saying, "My mother told me to tell you she isn't home this afternoon."

One particular Sunday morning the people noticed some cuts on the pastor's face. Also their patience was tested when he preached for 55 minutes.

One of the deacons spoke with the pastor after the service and asked him about the cuts.

Pastor: "This morning when I was shaving I was so worried about my sermon that I cut my face."

Deacon: "I suggest, Pastor, that in the future you be worried about your face and cut your sermon!"

The Indian chief had never attended a gospel service. When the revival came to a nearby town, he was persuaded to go and hear the evangelist. Afterwards a friend asked him: "How did you like the preacher?"

The chief answered: "Much wind, plenty of thunder, no rain!"

There was a knock on the door of the Methodist parsonage. When the minister opened the door a stranger informed him that his dog had died and he wondered if arrangements could be made for a funeral for the animal.

Methodist preacher: "I'm sorry about your loss, but really my schedule is so full I don't believe I could serve you at this time. Why don't you try the Baptist minister just 2 blocks down the street?"

Stranger: "Oh, thanks for the suggestion. Do you think I should give him a remuneration?"

Preacher: "Yes, I believe that would be in order."

Stranger: "Would a fee of $5,000 be about right?"

Preacher: "What's that? Just a minute! Why didn't you tell me that he was a *Methodist* dog?"

The minister asked his son, "Do you think the congregation reacted favorably to my sermon this morning?"

Son: "Yes, I'm sure they did, Dad. I saw several of them nodding all through your message."

In a message on the doctrine of Satan, the pastor called out, "And if there is anyone here who doesn't believe in a personal devil, just come up and see me after the service."

Deacon Anderson invariably went to sleep during the sermon. Pastor Johnson was upset and decided to rectify the situation. When Anderson was dozing, the pastor said in a calm voice, "All who want to go to heaven, please stand."

Everyone stood up, except the deacon. After

they were seated, the pastor said, "Now all who want to go to hell—please stand!" and yelled out the two words "please stand."

Quickly the sleeping man jumped to his feet. He looked around and sized up the situation and then spoke to the minister, "Pastor, I really don't know what we're voting on, but it looks like you and I are the only ones in favor of it."

Right in the middle of the service, just before the sermon, one of the choir members remembered she had forgotten to turn off the gas under the beef roast. Hurriedly she scribbled a note and gave it to an usher to take to her husband.

Unfortunately the usher misunderstood her and took it to the pulpit for the pastor. Unfolding the note he read: "Please go home and turn off the gas!"

The young preacher was flattered when a lady in the congregation shook his hand saying, "You are truly a model preacher." When he got to his office, he checked the meaning of the word *model*. He learned that *model* is "a small imitation of the real thing."

He strutted on to the platform, totally confident that he would amaze the audience with his powers of oratory, his homiletical genius, plus his mastery of vocabulary and syntax.

But the sermon bounced back in his face. The people were bored and unmoved. He felt humiliated. He came back to the parsonage as low as a snake's belly.

His wife put it this way: "If you went up to the pulpit the way you came down from the pulpit, you would have come down the way you went up."

Comment heard after the sermon: "That sermon went over like a lead balloon!"

(See also: Sermons, Church)

PRIDE

She came to the pastor's study saying she felt she ought to confess the sin of pride.

Pastor: "Yes, tell me all about it."

Lady: "I must confess that I just can't resist the temptation to sit in front of my mirror 2 or 3 hours every day admiring my beauty."

The pastor gave her a second look and then counseled her, "Well, it's not the sin of pride you need to confess; it's the sin of imagination!"

PROFESSORS

Student: "Were you out in all that rain, Professor?"

Professor: "No, I was merely in the portion of the rain that descended in my immediate vicinity."

Secretary: "Professor, isn't this the same exam you gave last year?"

Professor: "Yes, but I've changed the answers."

(See also: Absent-minded, College, Schools, Teachers)

PROPAGANDA

A little goose was receiving some information about his parents from a wise old goose. "Your mother," explained the scholarly bird, "is a propagoose, but your father is not a propaganda."

PROTESTORS

One protestor to his girl friend: "I'm on my way to pick up my unemployment check. Then I'll go over to the university office to see what's holding up this month's Federal Education Grant. Then I'll go and get this week's food stamps. Meanwhile you can go over to the Free Health Clinic and check up on your tests. I've got to drop around at the Welfare Department and demand our eligibility limit again. Then at 4 P.M. we'll meet at the Federal Building for another mass demonstration against this stinking, rotten *establishment!*"

PSYCHIATRISTS

Two psychiatrists met on the street. One smiled cheerfully and said, "Good morning!"

The other walked on and muttered to himself, "I wonder what he meant by that?"

The psychiatrist was reporting his findings to the husband of one of his patients. "I'm very sorry to have to give you this report, but your wife's mind is gone."

"I'm really not surprised," replied the husband. "She's been giving me a piece of it every day."

A man went to see a psychiatrist about his terrible memory. He said that if he was reading a book, he didn't dare lay it down for he would forget where he was reading, and what he was reading about. If in conversation, the conversation ceased for a moment, he couldn't remember what he had been talking about. Finally the doctor asked him when this condition started. "What condition?" was the reply.

Doctor to patient: "And what is your difficulty?"
Patient: "I just feel like a dog."
Doctor: "Yes, and how long have you felt that way?"
Patient: "Ever since I was a little puppy."

A neurotic is one who builds a castle in the air. A psychotic is one who lives in it. A psychiatrist is the one who collects the rent.

Anyone who goes to a psychiatrist ought to have his head examined. (Samuel Goldwyn)

124

Psychiatry enables us to correct our faults by confessing our parents' shortcomings.

PURPOSE

The unthinking child was asked a familiar catechism question, "What is the chief end of man?" And he answered, "The end with the head on."

QUAKERS

A pious Quaker was getting more and more upset with his cow as she kicked over the pail of milk, then swished her tail in his face. Finally while trying to maintain his sanctimonious composure he blurted out, "Cow, if thee does that again, this is what I will do with thee. I will sell thee to a Lutheran, who will know what to do with thy cursed tail and feet."

RESTAURANTS

On the wharf in San Francisco a man walked into a restaurant and asked, "Do you serve crabs?"

The waitress said quickly, "Sure, we serve anybody! Sit down!"

He was grouchy; he was demanding; he was impossible to please; but the waitress wanted to do her best to accommodate him. "Bring me two eggs," was his gruff order. "Boil one and scramble the other!"

A few minutes later she returned with his breakfast. When he looked at his plate he complained, "Take 'em back! You scrambled the wrong one!"

ROBBERS

Thieves were robbing a house one night when suddenly a chair was knocked over. The man of the house was awakened and he jumped out of bed and said, "What are you looking for?"

"Money," one robber replied.

127

"Well, turn on the light and I'll try to help you find some."

ROMANCE

Al: "Thelma, will you marry me?"
Thelma: "No, but I'll always admire your good taste."

Eve: "Adam, do you really love me?"
Adam: "Who else?"

Ward: "What would I have to give you for just one little kiss?"
Betty: "Chloroform!"

They call her "Appendix." If you take her out once, that's enough.

He sent his picture to the Lonely Hearts Club. The reply came back, "We're not that lonely."

Question: What do a patriot, a rooster, and an old maid have in common?
Answer: The parrot says, "Yankee doodle do."
The rooster says, "Cock-a-doodle do."
The old maid says, "Any dude'll do!"

She: "If you try to kiss me, I'll call my mother."
He: "Why not call your dad?"
She: "Oh, he isn't as deaf as my mother is."

She: "I just can't seem to learn to love you."
He: "But, darling, I've saved $20,000."
She: "Oh, give me one more lesson, quick!"

He: "Scientists have now discovered that people who live together for a long time eventually get to look alike."

She: "If that's the case, you may consider my refusal final."

Rosalyn: "I'll give you just thirty minutes to quit kissing me."

Father to young man downstairs: "Say, are you going to stay all night?"

George: "Just a minute, I'll call up my folks and see if they mind."

Dad, calling from upstairs to daughter: "Doesn't that young man down there know how to say good-night?"

Sandra: "I'll say he does."

Ollie, the young Swede, was on a date with his girl friend. The moon was full and bright. In that romantic setting Ollie said, "Ina, vill you be my vife?"

Ina: "Ya, Ollie, I vill be your vife."

Then there was silence, total silence for about 15 minutes. Finally Ina asked: "Ollie, vhy don't you say something?"

Ollie: "I tink I said too much already!"

"As I gaze into your limpid pools, how I'd like to take a swim."

David (on the telephone, talking with his girl friend): "Darling, there isn't a mountain I wouldn't climb in order to be with you. I would swim the widest stream or cross the burning desert. To be at your side I would go through floods and fire. So long, darling. I'll see you tomorrow—if it doesn't rain."

Angry Dad: "Tom, what do you mean by bringing my daughter home at 3:00 in the morning?"
Tom: "Well, it's this way: I have to be at school by 8:00 and a guy needs a few hours sleep!"

When a girl is single she has to stay up half the night waiting for her boyfriend to go home. After they are married she does the same thing —wait for him to *come* home!

Doug: "Do you like to roller skate?"
Darlene: "I love to."
Doug: "Oh, that's better than roller skating!"

Have you heard about the game called "Parlor Photography"? You turn out the lights and see what develops!

They were going to get married in about a week.
She: "Darling, there's something about me I've never told you and I think you should be aware of it before we are married. You see, I'm a vegetarian."
He: "Oh, that's OK. There's no problem. You just go to your church and I'll go to mine!"

Sam and Susie were out riding one afternoon and as they passed a farm with a flock of sheep,

Susie remarked, "I think sheep are the dumbest creatures alive."
Sam: "Yes, my lamb."

She: "Do you really love me, Paul?"
He: "You know I do, Mary."
She: "Do you love me enough to die for me?"
He: "Oh no, Mary, mine is an undying love."

Lois: "But surely you didn't tell Tony straight out that you love him, did you?"
Lynn: "Oh goodness no. He had to squeeze it out of me!"

They strolled down the lane together.
The sky was studded with stars.
They reached the gate together,
and he lifted for her the bars.
She raised her brown eyes to him.
There was nothing between them now.
But he was just a farmer boy,
and she—a Jersey cow.

Did you hear about the manicurist who fell in love with a pedicurist and they were married?
They are waiting on each other hand and foot.

She: "Am I the only girl you have ever kissed?"
He: "Yes, and by far the prettiest."

Sarah had just broken off her engagement with the young doctor.

"Do you mean to tell me," exclaimed her girl friend, "that he actually asked you to return all his presents?"

"Not only that," Sarah replied, "but he also sent me a bill for 43 house calls!"

Elaine: "Is it really true that you'll commit suicide if I don't marry you?"
Phil: "Yes, that's been my custom down through the years."

Cliff to Jeannie: "If you'll only marry me just this once, I'll do the same for you someday."

He and she at basketball game.
He: "See that big fellow on the bench. He's only a freshman this year, but I think he's going to be our best man next year."
She: "Oh, darling, this is so sudden!"

SALESMEN

Salesman to customer: "This is actually a fire sale. If I don't make a sale, I'm fired!"

SATAN

A mother had insisted that Jackie not go swimming. When he came home with his hair wet she knew he had disobeyed.

Mother: "Jackie, shame on you! You've disobeyed me! Didn't I tell you that if Satan tempted you to disobey me that you should tell him to get behind you?"

Jackie: "But Mommy that's what I did. I was standing there on the river bank, and when I was tempted to go swimming I told Satan to get behind me . . . and when he got behind me, he just pushed me right into the water!"

SATIRE

I call my wife liberty bell because she is half-cracked.

Use your head. It's the little things that count!

She has a sense of direction like an eggbeater.

Some people cause happiness wherever they go; others cause happiness *whenever* they go.

Why don't you come over and have dinner, if you don't mind imposing?

At a banquet a lovely woman was seated between a Jewish rabbi on her right and a Presbyterian pastor on her left.

    She made the observation, "I sort of feel like a leaf between the Old and New Testaments."

    To which the rabbi replied, "That page, Madam, is usually blank."

Some folks sit and think, others just sit.

You must be twins. No one guy could be so dumb.

I don't know what's eating her, but I predict it will suffer from indigestion.

He has a chip on his shoulder: his head!

You look like the advance agent for a panic.

If the government had a tax on brains it would owe you money.

Think! There simply must be a harder way to do it.

You have one bad habit: you breathe.

I would like to help you out: which door will you use?

If you can keep your head in all this confusion, you simply don't know the situation.

You're certainly trying: *very* trying!

Diplomacy Department: We do and say the nastiest things in the nicest way!

We can't always be wrong . . . but we keep trying.

He not only encroaches on your time . . . he trespasses on eternity.

He has no equal in keeping a conversation "ho humming."

He's as stimulating as a mouthful of sawdust.

We don't know what we would do without you, but it would surely be fun to find out.

We have no quarrel with competitors who sell for less . . . after all they know what their merchandise is worth.

You should go far; and I hope very soon.

Of course our coffee tastes like mud. It was ground this morning.

There is no good reason for it. It's just our policy.

My mind is already made up, so don't confuse me with the facts.

I am never interested in anything until I find out it's none of my business.

Be sure to work 8 hours—and sleep 8 hours—but not the *same* 8 hours!

He'll go thundering down through history like an extra quart of water going over Niagara Falls.

If all else fails, try following directions.

If you can't convince 'em, confuse 'em.

Are you looking for someone with a little authority? I have as little as anyone.

I wish I had a lower I.Q. so I could enjoy a conversation with you.

He is always able to keep his head above water. That's because wood floats!

Look, I refuse to engage in a battle of wits with you. It's my policy never to attack anyone who is unarmed.

He has a concrete mind—permanently set and all mixed up.

He's a man of rare intelligence: It's rare when he shows any.

She is so obstinate and contrary that if she drowned they'd look upstream for her.

SARCASM
What's on your mind? . . . if you will please excuse the exaggeration.

She is such a lousy housekeeper that when you leave her place you feel you should wipe your feet.

He can stay longer in an *hour* than most people do in a *week*.

When he was born his father chose to call him "Theophilus" (Acts 1:1). When friends asked him why that name, the father's reply was, "He's got theophilus face I've ever seen."

He left his job because of illness and fatigue. . . . His boss got sick and tired of him.

He's mean, selfish, loudmouthed and uncouth, but in spite of all that there's something about him that simply repels you.

SCHOOL
Student to teacher: "I don't think I deserve an 'F' on my report card for this subject."

Teacher: "I agree with you, but that's the lowest mark there is."

Teacher: "Frank, is the word *trousers* singular or plural?"
Frank (after a long pause): "Singular at the top and plural at the bottom."

Little Gary came home after his first day of school.
Mother: "How did you like it, Gary?"
Gary: "Oh, I have to go back again tomorrow because I haven't learned how to read and write yet."

Teacher: "David, where do the bugs go in the winter time?"
David: "Search me."

Eight-year-old to teacher: "I don't want to scare you, but my daddy says if I don't get better grades, somebody's gonna get spanked."

Dad (looking over his son's report card): "One thing is certain—with grades like this, you sure haven't been cheating!"

Teacher: "Name 2 pronouns."
Student: "Who? Me?"

Don't like the teacher,
the subject's too deep.
I'd cut the class,
but I need the sleep!

I can't read this during the daytime.
You see I went to *night* school!

Glen: "Say, Dad, do you know how lucky you
are?"
Dad: "No, why?"
Glen: "You won't have to buy any new books
for me next fall. I'm going to take this past
year's work over again!"

Chemistry teacher: "Dan, what is the formula
for water?"
Dan: "It's H, I, J, K, L, M, N, O."
Teacher: "That's not the formula *I* gave you."
Dan: "Sure it is. You said the formula for water
is H to O."

Teddy was in third grade. He asked his dad to
help him with his homework, but his dad wasn't
very interested.

Whereupon the wife said, "Ed, you'd better
help him while you still can. Remember next
year he goes into fourth grade!"

For the third straight time, Andy brought home
a terrible report card. After reading it with
dismay, his dad signed it with an X.

Andy asked, "Why did you do that?"

His dad answered, "I don't want the teacher
to think that anyone with marks like that has
a father who can read and write."

A mother was having a hard time getting her
son to go to school one morning.

139

"Nobody likes me at school," said the son. "The teachers don't and the kids don't. The superintendent wants to transfer me, the bus drivers hate me. I don't want to go."

"But John, you've got to go," insisted the mother. "You're not sick. It isn't raining. You're supposed to be there. They are expecting you. And what's more you are now 45 years old and the principal of the school—you simply must go!"

A teacher in California suggested that her sixth graders imitate a session of the United Nations. One of the youngsters volunteered to represent Russia. It was soon understood why he chose Russia, for as the session got underway, the "Russian" delegate promptly got up and walked out of the room. (Frank Freeman)

The English teacher was doing everything possible to urge the students to augment and enrich their vocabulary. He told the class, "If you repeat a word 8 or 10 times, I assure you, it will be yours for all your life."

In the back row Sally closed her blue eyes and muttered softly to herself, "Steve, Steve, Steve."

(See also: College, Professors, Teachers)

SCOTSMEN

A notice in a church bulletin in Glasgow had this to say: "Some are putting buttons in the church offering. Please, if you do so, bring your own buttons. Don't detach buttons from the cushions of the church pews for this purpose."

John sent an indignant letter to the editor of the local newspaper. "If there appear any more stories about stingy Scotsmen in the columns of your paper, I'm going to stop borrowing the paper from my neighbor."

SECRET

I can keep a secret but the folks I tell it to can't.

SELF

How disappointing when they say,
"I didn't know you'd been away."

SERMONS

"If all who have gone to sleep during my sermons were put end to end, they would be more comfortable!"

"My sermons are not long, they just seem long."

A stranger entered the church during the sermon and sat down on the back row. Leaning over to an elderly man he asked: "How long has he been preaching?"
Old-timer: "About 40 years I think."
Stranger: "I'll stay then—he must be nearly finished."

141

Pastor Reynolds was getting into the habit of preaching longer and longer—55 minutes and even an hour or longer. At the deacon meeting, the chairman tried to be very diplomatic in suggesting that the pastor preach shorter messages.

"But," the pastor explained, "don't you realize I'm giving you the milk of the Word?"

"Yes, Pastor," replied the chairman, "but in the future we suggest you give us *condensed milk!*"

A sermon can help people in different ways. Some rise from a sermon greatly strengthened; others wake from it delightfully refreshed.

Deacon Sandberg nearly always went to sleep during the morning sermon. His wife was so embarrassed she desperately sought a solution. A friend suggested she take a piece of Limburger cheese, wrap it in a piece of tissue and have it ready the next Sunday.

Predictably her husband started nodding about 10 minutes into the sermon. So she quietly removed the cheese from her purse and carefully passed it beneath his nose. Whereupon the deacon was heard to murmur, "No, Mary, no—don't kiss me now, Mary!"

(See also: Church, Preachers)

SICKNESS

A hypochondriac told his doctor in great alarm that he was certain he had a fatal liver disease.

"Nonsense!" protested the doctor. "You wouldn't know whether you had that or not. With that particular disease, there's no discomfort of any kind."

"Good heavens!" the patient gasped. "My symptoms exactly!"

SIGN

Sign seen in a kitchen: "The views expressed by the husband are not necessarily those of the management."

Signs seen in an office:
"I'd like to compliment you on your work. When will you start?"

"You don't have to be crazy to work here, but it helps!"

Motel sign: Inn Mates Wanted.

Bakery sign: We Discovered Our Roll in Life.

Sign in custom's office: Customs Inspectors Know Their Duties.

Sign in canoe rental shop: "No Tipping Allowed."

SIMILES

As helpless as the owner of a sick goldfish.

SINGING

I only sing for my own amazement.

She has a good range, but I wish she would keep it in her kitchen.

SINGLES

An unmarried woman should never be called an "old maid." She should be referred to as "a monument to some man's utter stupidity."

A 20-year-old daughter earnestly prayed before climbing into bed: "Dear God, I don't ask anything for myself, but I do pray for my mother. Please give mother a handsome son-in-law."

SMILE-A-GRAMS

Women like the simpler things of life—*men*.

Your tongue weighs practically nothing. So how come you can't hold it?

Come in, we were expecting you . . . everything else has gone wrong today.

SMOKING

Non-smoker to smoker: "I don't smoke, but I do chew. So let's have an understanding. If you don't blow your smoke on me, then I won't spit on you!"

SO DUMB

Note: There are Polish jokes, Hollander jokes, Spanish jokes, etc. The following are listed under the title "So Dumb." Go ahead and adapt them in any way you wish.

Did you hear about the dummy who read that most accidents occur within two miles of home? So he moved away!

Teacher: "Dummy, where do you live?"
Dummy: "With my brother."
Teacher: "Yes, but where does *he* live?"
Dummy: "He lives with me."
Teacher (disgusted): "But where do the two of you live?"
Dummy: "We live with each other."

The doctor told him he should avoid all dampness because of his rheumatism. Thereafter he could be found every night in the bathtub going over himself with a vacuum cleaner!

They are so dumb that the *Coca Cola* distributors have to put a notice on the bottom of each bottle, "Open other end."

Then there was the dummy who continued driving around the block until he had done it 17 times. His directional turn lever had stuck.

And did you hear about the fellow who bought an AM radio? After using it for 2 weeks he discovered it also worked in the PM.

"Why does it take 5 dummys to pop popcorn?"
  "One has to hold the pan and four are needed to jiggle the stove."

She is so dumb she thinks hold up men are swimming instructors.

He is so dumb he can't work up a good headache.

They are so dumb that they need the letters "t-g-i-f" stamped on their shoes, meaning *toes go in first*.

They are so dumb they think that *assets* are *little donkeys*.

He is so dumb he cut a hole in the boat and then plugged it with a cork. That way he could drain the water out!

He is so dumb he thinks South Bend is a morning sitting up exercise and that Lansing, Michigan, is major surgery.

He is so dumb he thinks you have to put on a swimsuit to go into a pool room.

He is so dumb he thinks that Dan and Beersheba are husband and wife—just like Sodom and Gomorrah.

He is so dumb he thinks a blizzard is the inside of a fowl and that a goblet is a little turkey.

Then there was the fellow who took a bale of hay to bed with him—so he could feed his night-mare!

George wasn't too bright, and the gang liked to pick on him. One day they showed him a huge watermelon and bet him 50¢ he couldn't eat it all at one session.

Before venturing, however, George hurried home. Returning some 15 minutes later, he proceeded to demolish the whole melon without stopping.

"Why did you go home first, George?" they asked him.

"Mom had a bigger melon in the kitchen, and I knew if I could eat it, I could eat this smaller one."

Caller: "Long distance. I want to place a call to Damariscota, Maine."

Telephone operator: "How do you spell that please?"

Caller: "Listen, lady, if I could spell it, I'd be writing, not phoning."

My parents are in the iron and steel business. Mom irons and Dad steals.

Mick: "I have a cold or something in my head."

Jack: "Must be a cold."

SPEAKERS
The after-dinner speaker was handed a note just before he was due to speak. It was from his wife and said simply, "Kiss, Betty."

The lady sitting next to him remarked, "How sweet of your wife to remind you of her love just before you have to make an important speech."

"That isn't quite the message," he explained. "What this note means is 'Keep it short, stupid!' "

You can't tell whether a man is a finished speaker until he sits down.

A valuable guideline for public speakers: If you don't strike oil in 20 minutes stop boring!

There are 3 rules for public speakers.
1. Stand up to be seen.
2. Speak up to be heard.
3. Shut up to be appreciated.

At a noonday men's luncheon the speaker inquired of the toastmaster, "How much time shall I take?"

Toastmaster: "No problem, just talk as long as you want to, but the rest of us will be leaving at 1:00!"

The men's fellowship consisted of two parts: first a time of informal fellowship and then the message from the guest speaker. The chairman was trying to bring the first part to a conclusion and called out, "Hey, fellows, let's come to order. It's time for the speaker. You can enjoy yourselves some other time."

A pastor was trying to make a very flowery introduction of the guest speaker. "Friends, from time to time we have men of great renown come to speak to us, and it has been our privilege to have men of high positions ministering to us. We are thankful for those of outstanding rank who have visited us, but this morning we have the rankest of them all!"

He needs no introduction. What he needs is a conclusion.

Advice to speakers: "Please keep in mind that the mind cannot absorb more than the seat can endure."

He had the ability to speak for an entire hour—without any notes, and without a single point.

Mike's dad took him to an alumni banquet at Yale University. The speaker used the letters Y-A-L-E for his speech:

    Y—for youth
    A—for ambition
    L—for loyalty
    E—for enthusiasm

and he spent about 20 minutes on each point. During the last point, Mike whispered to his dad, "I'm sure glad you didn't attend the Massachusetts Institute of Technology!"

SPEECH

A farmer in South Carolina left home at 9 A.M. driving his mules to town. He got home several hours late and his wife started to tongue-lash him for taking so long.

He explained, "A half hour down the road this morning the preacher hitched a ride with me. From that time on those lousy mules couldn't understand a word I said."

SUCCESS

The Lord has given us two ends,
  they have a common link;
For with the bottom end we sit,
  and with the other think.
Success in life depends upon
  which end you choose to use.
You'll soon discover this, my friend,
  Heads you win and *tails* you lose!

SUMMER CAMP

Bobby wrote a letter home from summer camp. It read, "Please send me food—all they serve here is breakfast, lunch and dinner."

SUNDAY SCHOOL

Teacher: "Now girls, tell me, what are the sins of omission?"
Mary: "I think they are the sins we ought to have committed, but haven't."

Paul came home from Sunday school and his mother asked him if he could repeat the memory verse. "Oh sure," he replied, "it's the verse that says, 'A lie is an abomination unto the Lord, but an ever present help in time of trouble.' "

The lesson in Sunday school was on Jonah and the whale. When the teacher had finished she asked, "And now, Charles, can you tell us what lesson this story teaches us?"

"Yes," answered Charles, "it teaches that you can't keep a good man down!"

It was promotion Sunday for the Sunday school.
Teacher: "Who can tell me what special day this is?"
Youngster: "I know! It's commotion Sunday."
(F. W. Roseburg)

The lesson was on getting victory over sin. "Now, Billy," the teacher questioned, "tell me what must we do before we can expect forgiveness of sin?"

There was a moment's thought, then Billy replied, "We gotta sin."

The Sunday school teacher was describing how Lot's wife looked back and turned into a pillar of salt, when little Jimmy interrupted. "My mother looked back once while she was driving," he announced triumphantly, "and she turned into a telephone pole!"

Asked what he'd learned at Sunday school, the 10-year-old began, "Well, our teacher told us about when God sent Moses behind the enemy

151

lines to rescue the Israelites from the Egyptians. When they came to the Red Sea, Moses called for the engineers to build a pontoon bridge. After they had all crossed, they looked back and saw the Egyptian tanks coming. Quick as a flash, Moses radioed headquarters on his walkie-talkie to send bombers to blow up the bridge and save the Israelites."

"Bobby," exclaimed his startled mother, "is that really the way your teacher told that story?"

"Well, not exactly. But if I told it her way, you'd never believe it!"

A Sunday school teacher said to Willie: "What are you drawing, Willie?"
Willie: "A picture of God."
Teacher: "But Willie, don't you realize that nobody knows how God looks?"
Willie: "Well, they will when I get this done."

SWEDES

Gustav Nelson: "I yused to live in United States, but aye tink I go bak to Minnesota."

Ollie brought his horse to a horse auction. John Hayward saw the horse and said, "Ollie, I want to buy your horse."

"Vell, he no look good," responded Ollie.

"Oh, we can curry him—there'll be no problem."

"But he no look good," objected the Swede.

Mr. Hayward repeated that things would be

OK, so he paid Ollie the price and went on his way with the horse.

Fifteen minutes later he returned and was infuriated. "Ollie," he shouted, "you're a scoundrel, a crook! That horse you sold me is blind!"

"Vell," countered Ollie, "I told you, he no *look* good!"

Our Swedish friend had fallen and broken her hip in Quito, Ecuador. During her healing process a Spanish-speaking assistant put a heating pad on her hip, but after a few moments it got unbearably hot.

She told of her experience to a visitor later saying, "I jelled and I jelled and jelled, but nobody came—because I jelled 'yelp' in English, when I should have jelled 'yelp' in Spanish."

TALK

She talks like a book,
her admirers all say.
What a pity she can't be
shut up the same way.

She hitched a caboose on my train of thought.

She's the kind that talks on and on about things
that leave her speechless.

Trying to get a word in edgewise with some
people is like trying to thread a sewing machine
with the motor running.

She lets her mind go blank, but forgets to turn
off the sound.

TAXES

It seems a little silly now, but this country
was founded as a protest against high taxes.

Tax collector: "Why don't you pay your taxes with a smile?"

Walter Barnes: "That's a great idea, but you always insist on money!"

TEACHERS

The teacher wrote on the chalkboard, "I ain't had no fun this summer at all." Then she asked a youngster in her class, "Susan, what would you suggest that I do to correct that statement?"

Susan studied the sentence for a moment and then replied, "Get another boyfriend!"

Teacher: "Which is more important to us—the moon or the sun?"

Johnny: "The moon."

Teacher: "Why?"

Johnny: "The moon gives us light at night when we need it, the sun gives us light only in the day when we don't need it."

Peter: "Should a person be punished for something he hasn't done?"

Teacher: "No, certainly not."

Peter: "That's good, because I haven't done my arithmetic."

A teacher had told her class that Milton, the poet, was blind; so she put the question on the next day's literature quiz: "What was Milton's affliction?" About half the class filled in the blank with "poet."

Did you hear about the cross-eyed school teacher? She couldn't control her pupils.

Teacher to mother about her child: "Don't believe everything he tells you about me and I won't believe everything he tells me about you."

A teacher was at the end of her rope with Willie. Finally she wrote a note to the mother: "Your son is the brightest boy in the class, but he is also the most mischievous. What shall I do?"

The mother's reply was: "Do as you please —I'm having my own troubles with his father."

Teacher: "Wally, how would you divide 9 potatoes equally among 6 people?"
Wally: "I'd mash 'em!"

(See also: College, Professors, Schools)

TEEN-AGER
Teen-ager: "Dad could you go to a P.T.A. meeting tonight? It's sort of a private P.T.A. meeting . . . just you, me and the principal."

The young couple had found a secluded spot in a quiet woodland glade but failed to notice the "Private Keep Out" sign.

Presently, the owner came along, bristling with rage, and confronted the lovers. "Can't you read?" he demanded.

The girl blushed, but the young man was equal to the occasion. "Oh, yes," he said, "but we didn't bring a book."

A teen-ager was making application for a job. The employer asked: "What makes you think you are responsible?"

Teen-ager: "On every job I've ever had so far, whenever anything went wrong, the boss would say to me, 'You're responsible!' "

TELEPHONES

The bathtub was invented in 1850 and the telephone in 1875. Just think—if you had been living in 1850 you could have taken baths for 25 years without the phone ringing once!

TEMPERANCE

The temperance lecturer was illustrating the evils of liquor. Dramatically producing 2 glasses, one filled with water and the other filled with whiskey he proceeded to drop a live worm into each glass. The worm in the water swam around in a lively manner, while the one in the whiskey promptly curled up and died.

"Now then," he exclaimed triumphantly, "what does this prove?"

"If you drink whiskey, you won't have worms," replied Morry.

TEMPTATION

The average number of times people say, "No" to temptation is once weakly.

"It seems like I can resist everything except temptation."

What makes resisting temptation difficult, for most people, is that they don't want to discourage it completely.

TEXANS

A rangy Texan was getting acquainted with a fellow in Minneapolis.

"Do you own any land in Texas?" asked the northerner.

"Oh, a little bit," answered the Texan.

"How many acres?"

"Only three acres."

"That's pretty small. Where are they?"

"In the middle of downtown Dallas."

A Texan and a Kentuckian were trying to outdo the other in boasting about their respective states.

The fellow from Kentucky bragged, "In my state we have enough gold to build a solid gold fence, 3 feet high and 2 feet wide, all the way around Texas."

"Good idea," replied the Texan. "Go ahead and build it. If we like it, we'll buy it."

A young Texan moved to Chicago where he constantly told his friends about the greatness of his state. No matter what the category, he always found a way to claim that Texans were first, the Texans were the greatest, etc.

His Chicago friends got tired of all the boasting and decided to play a prank on the Texan. When he was asleep they gave him a small dose of ether to guarantee he would stay asleep for awhile. They borrowed a casket from the funeral home and put him in it. Then they took him out to the cemetery placing the casket and its occupant alongside a freshly dug grave. They hid behind the bushes to watch what would happen.

A half hour later the Texan started to open his eyes. Yawning and looking around him, he noticed the casket, the tombstones, the open grave and he began to shout, "Amen! Hallelujah! Praise the Lord! The day of resurrection has come and what do you think—we Texans are the first ones out!"

She was a Texan hostess performing her "howdy duties."

At a breakfast in a south Texas hotel I ordered hot cakes smothered in melted butter.

"We only serve margarine here," said the waitress.

"I can't understand it," I said with some annoyance. "Here we've driven hundreds of miles across wonderful grazing land and have

been told time and again that the finest cattle
in the world are raised right here. Why don't
you serve butter?"

"Ma'am," she said, "here in Texas we ride
'em and we eat 'em . . . we don't milk 'em!"
(Mrs. William A. Rutzen)

A Texan was visiting Niagara Falls.
Guide: "I'll bet you don't have anything like
this in Texas."
Texan: "Nope, I reckon we don't. But we've
got plumbers who could fix it."

THANKSGIVING

Husband (as they sat down to eat): "Honey,
this turkey is beautiful. And tell me what
kind of stuffing did you use?"
Young wife: "Stuffing? I didn't use any stuffing
—this turkey wasn't hollow!"

TRAFFIC

On the streets of Chicago there are 2 kinds
of pedestrians—"the quick and the dead."

Be a patient pedestrian—otherwise you'll be a
pedestrian patient!

TRAINS

A big executive boarded a New York to Chicago
train. He explained to the porter: "I'm a heavy
sleeper and I want you to be sure to wake me

at 3:00 A.M. to get off at Buffalo. Regardless of what I say, get me up, and get me off the train. I may resist you, but I've got to get off at Buffalo."

But the next morning the executive awakened just as the train pulled into Chicago. He was infuriated, and he really poured it on the porter with abusive language.

As he stomped down the platform toward the station another passenger asked the porter, "How could you stand there and take that kind of talk from that fellow?"

The porter replied, "That was nothing. You should have heard what the man said that I put off in Buffalo!"

Two fellows were taking a train trip together through a mountainous area. Both had lunches including a banana in each. They came to a tunnel. A few seconds after entering it the first fellow called to his friend, "Don't eat your banana! I started eating mine and I immediately went blind!"

TRUTH

Beware of half-truth: You may have gotten the wrong half.

UNDERTAKER

Newspaper ad for a funeral director: "We'll be the last ones to let you down!"

USELESSNESS

A fellow and his wife went to an amusement park. He wanted to go on the merry-go-round. She thought it was silly. So he got on alone.

When he had finished she nagged him. "Now look at you! You've spent all your money; you get right off where you got on; and you ain't been nowhere!"

USHERS

The wife of the bank president came into a church a little late and was about to be seated in a pew that was supposed to be reserved. The usher became very flustered as he tried to explain. What came out was: "I meg your bardon, padam, but this pie is occu-pewed. May I sew you to another sheet?"

VALENTINE'S DAY

(See: Romance)

VISITORS

A wife's complaint: "If there's anything that upsets me, it's having people drop in when the house looks the way it usually does."

Make yourself right at home—and we sure wish you were!

Your visit has climaxed an already very dull day.

Hostess (as her guests lingered on and on): "I sure wish they had some get up and go!"

WEATHER

Did you hear the weather report for Latin America today? It's to be Chile today and hot tamale!

It was raining cats and dogs and leaving little poodles.

WEDDINGS

After the ceremony the groom asked the preacher, "How much is the fee?"

Pastor: "There's no set fee—just whatever you think she's worth."

The groom handed him a $1 bill.

The pastor took another look at the bride, and then pulled out 2 quarters from his pocket, handing them to the fellow saying, "Here's your change!"

Did you hear about the 2 octopuses that got married? They came down the aisle arm in arm . . . arm in arm . . . arm in arm.

"Doesn't the bride look stunning?"
"Yes, and doesn't the groom look stunned?"

Three words dominate the bride's thinking during the wedding march: *Aisle—altar—hymn.*

A couple made arrangements with the pastor to celebrate their wedding ceremony at the close of the Sunday morning service. So when he had finished his sermon he announced, "Those desiring to be married may now come to the front." Seventeen women and one man came!

Harry: "I sure got an awful fright at my wedding."
Larry: "You did?"
Harry: "Yes, I still have her."

A young preacher became very flustered at his first wedding. At the conclusion of the ceremony he said, "The audience will now come forward and view the remains."

In the wedding ceremony they came to the spot where the father was to give the bride away.
Minister: "And now, who gives this woman to be married to this man?"
Father: "My mother and I do!"

(See also: Husbands, Marriage, Wives)

WHAT?

Q: What did one ear say to the other?
A: *I didn't know we lived on the same block.*

Q: What does an elephant do when he hurts his toe?
A: *He calls a tow truck.*

Q: What do you get when you cross a goat with an owl?
A: *A hootenanny.*

Q: What did the boy octopus say to the girl octopus?
A: *Let me hold your hand, hand, hand, hand, hand, hand, hand, hand.*

Q: What do they call a man who steals ham?
A: *A hamburglar.*

Q: What is practical nursing?
A: *Falling in love with a rich patient.*

Q: What do they call a bull that sleeps a lot?
A: *A bulldozer.*

Q: What is a 5-year-old African girl who poisons her mother and father?
A: *An orphan.*

WHY?

Q: Why does Santa Claus have 3 gardens?
A: *So he can "ho, ho, ho."*

Q: Why don't ducks fly backward?
A: *The tail's on the wrong end.*

Q: Why do elephants have wrinkles?
A: *Have you ever tried to iron one?*

WIVES

Ralph and Ray were talking about their wives.
Ralph: "Is your wife entertaining this week?"
Ray: "No, not very!"

Whenever my wife needs money, she calls me "handsome." She says, "Hand some over."

Hubby: "What did you say?"
Wife: "Nothing."
Hubby: "Of course, but how did you express it this time?"

Margaret: "It just can't be that I have overdrawn our checking account. I still have several blank checks left!"

Three fellows got married the same summer.
John married Pearl and got a jewel.
Art married Violet and got a flower.
Larry married Hazel and got a nut.

Kevin: "My wife is an angel."
Nelson: "What do you mean?"
Kevin: "First, she's always up in the air. Second, she harps on one string; and third, she doesn't have an earthly thing to wear!"

His wife was sick in bed, and he was trying to fix breakfast, but things were in a mess. The tea was missing. He looked high and low, but no tea could he find.

Finally he called to his wife, "I can't find the tea anywhere. Where do you keep it?"

She answered, "I don't know why you can't find it. It's right there on the cupboard shelf—in a cookie tin marked 'matches.'"

A wife complained to her doctor, "I am afraid that my husband has some terrible mental affliction. Sometimes I talk to him for hours and then discover he literally hasn't heard a word I said."

"That isn't an affliction," was the physician's reply, "that's a divine gift!"

"The doctor said that my wife and I need more exercise, so I've just bought myself a set of golf clubs," said Larry to his neighbor.

"That's good. And what have you bought for your wife?"

"A lawn mower."

(See also: Husbands, Marriage, Weddings)

WOMEN

"I'm at a bad time in my life," she said.

"Why?"

"Well I'm too young for Medicare and I'm too old for 'men-to-care.'"

She says she has absolutely nothing to wear—and she needs 3 closets to keep it in.

Her hat looks like it had made a forced landing on her head.

A dignified-looking, middle-aged gentleman decided to take advantage of a special sale and buy his wife a pair of nylons. After waiting about an hour on the fringe of a screaming, pushing mob of women, he plunged toward the counter with both arms flying.

Suddenly a shrill voice hollered out, "Can't you act like a gentleman?"

"I've been acting like a gentleman for over an hour and it got me nowhere," he replied, still plowing toward the counter. "Now, I'm going to act like a lady!"

Mary: "I ran into Betty today. I hadn't seen her in years."
Virginia: "Tell me, has she kept her girlish figure?"
Mary: "Kept it? She's doubled it!"

She'd be more "spick" if she had less "span."

Jeannie: "Bernie, don't forget to bring home another mousetrap."
Bernie: "What's the matter with the one I bought yesterday?"
Jeannie: "It's full now."

Allen: "Hey, there won't be any women in
    heaven."
Alfred: "How come?"
Allen: "I was just reading in Revelation 8:1 that
    for a half hour there was silence in heaven."

Four women in Kansas got into a terrible
argument. After much yelling, screaming, and
pulling of hair, one of them called out, "I'm
on my way to the sheriff to report you."

The other three wanted to get there first.
What resulted was all four rushed into his office,
each trying to be the first to relate her
complaints. Charges and countercharges filled
the air.

The sheriff called for order. When quiet had
been restored, he showed some of Solomon's
wisdom when he announced, "All right ladies,
I'll hear one at a time. The oldest can speak
first."

That closed the case.

A lady was visiting a mink farm in Maine. She
asked the employee: "How many pelts do you
get off these little animals?"

Employee: "Well, lady, we find that if we skin
them more than once a year it makes the
animals very nervous."

She's in her early flirties.

She's stopped exercising—pushing 50 is all the
exercise she can take.

She says things she hasn't even thought of as yet.

Amy: "Whenever I'm down in the dumps, I get a new dress."
Norma: "I've wondered where you got them."

It happened in a travel agency. Two middle-aged ladies instructed the agent: "We'd like to get completely away from civilization—you know, near some nice shopping district."

WORDS

He never opens his mouth unless he has nothing to say.

She must have been vaccinated with a phonograph needle.

Her vocabulary is small, but the turnover is terrific.

WORK

All work and no play makes Jack a dull boy— and Jill a wealthy widow.

One of the greatest labor-saving inventions of today is tomorrow.

If you don't want to work you have to work to earn enough money so that you won't have to work. (Ogden Nash)

Most people like hard work. Especially when they are the ones paying for it.

WORRY

A famous preacher was asked if he worried. "Oh, of course not," he answered, "Because worry is sin—and if I'm going to sin, I would choose something that's a lot more fun."

Mamie: "Roberta, you've got to stop your worrying. It doesn't do a bit of good."
Roberta: "Oh, yes it does! Ninety percent of the things I worry about never happen!"

WRITING

I love being a writer. What I can't stand is the paperwork. (Peter De Vries)

ZEAL

Keep your eye on the ball, your shoulder to
the wheel, your ear to the ground, and your
nose to the grindstone. Now try to work in that
position!